13   12   79

The POWER Series

DELTA

America's Elite Counterterrorist Force

Terry Griswold and D. M. Giangreco

Motorbooks International
Publishers & Wholesalers ®

First published in 1992 by Motorbooks International
Publishers & Wholesalers, PO Box 2, 729 Prospect Avenue,
Osceola, WI 54020 USA

The information in this book is true and complete to the
best of our knowledge. All recommendations are made
without any guarantee on the part of the author or Publisher,
who also disclaim any liability incurred in connection with
the use of this data or specific details

We recognize that some words, model names and
designations, for example, mentioned herein are the
property of the trademark holder. We use them for
identification purposes only. This is not an official
publication

Motorbooks International books are also available at
discounts in bulk quantity for industrial or sales-promotional
use. For details write to Special Sales Manager at the
Publisher's address

Library of Congress Cataloging-in-Publication Data
Griswold, Terry A.
    Delta, America's elite counterterrorist force / Terry A.
Griswold, D.M. Giangreco.
      p.   cm. — (The Power series)
    Includes index.
    ISBN 0-87938-615-0
    1. United States. Army. Delta Force—History.   2.
Special forces (Military science)—United States—
History—20th century.
3. Terrorism—United States—History—20th
century. I. Giangreco, D. M., 1952-   II.
Title.   III. Series: Power series (Osceola, Wis.)
UA34.S64G75 1992
356'.16'0973—dc20   92-9008

On the front cover: A DELTA trooper practices a
surprise entry through a window after rappelling down the side of a building.
On the back cover: Top, DELTA training is
always as realistic as possible; here an assault team
"picks" a lock with C4 plastic explosives. Bottom,
a trooper prepares to toss a flash/bang grenade
during training. Note his specially equipped
H&K MP5 submachine gun.

Printed in Hong Kong

Contents

Preface   6

Chapter 1: Out of the Desert   8

Chapter 2: A New Game in Town   20

    Weapons and Equipment   32

Chapter 3: The Making of a DELTA Trooper   40

Chapter 4: Decade of Frustration   60

    Air Support: Rotary- and Fixed-Wing Assets   78

Chapter 5: Back to the Desert   92

Chapter 6: The Scud Busters   106

Epilogue   124

Index   128

Preface

This is another type of war, new in its intensity, ancient in its origins—war by guerrillas, subversives, insurgents, assassins . . . seeking victory by eroding and exhausting the enemy instead of engaging him.

President John F. Kennedy, 1962

The success of Fidel Castro's Cuban revolution in 1959 and rising tide of insurgencies around the globe made it clear to newly elected President of the United States John F. Kennedy that the focus of communist expansionism had shifted to the Third World. Kennedy firmly believed that the communist's ominous Cuban foothold in the Western Hemisphere could be countered by a program aimed at stimulating peaceful evolution instead of violent revolution. His response to the communists' challenge was the Alliance for Progress.

The Alliance for Progress was a serious effort to promote stability in Latin America through political reform, as well as economic and social development, and it served as a model for similar US commitments in other less–developed regions. Embryonic communist insurgencies threatened this evolutionary process, and Kennedy moved quickly to blunt their threat by devising and implementing a doctrine of counterrevolutionary warfare. More than thirty years later, the descendants

of his elite, unconventional warriors continue to assist dozens of potential or fledgling democracies while specifically tasked, direct–action arms of the Army, Navy, and Air Force stand ready to fight an insidious by–product of Third World instability and the recent Cold War: terrorism.

In the years following the Iran hostage crisis and disaster at *Desert I*, a great deal has been written on the 1st Special Forces Operational Detachment–DELTA. Most of the focus has been on the origins of the failed rescue attempt, the major players, technical problems, and in some cases, the strategic and tactical leadership of the units involved. However, the guts and backbone of DELTA and similar units is the individual trooper. For the most part, he is typical of those in the special operations community.

But there is more to the soldiers who make up DELTA. Each man is a self–starter who not only displays personal initiative but can work well when part of a team. They are mature individuals, confident in themselves and their unit, who are unquestioned experts in their craft. These qualities are more than just factors in what makes a good DELTA trooper, they are the essence of DELTA. And while most of the unit's officers stay around long enough to learn the art of counterterrorist (CT) operations, it is still the old hands, the highly professional noncommissioned and warrant officers, that keep DELTA on the straight and narrow. This story examines CT training and operations from their viewpoint: the elite special operations team members who must wade into the dirty business of counterterrorism to protect US lives and interests.

In a free—and financially strapped—society, there is immense pressure on units costing the taxpayer millions of dollars to produce and show results. Because of the clandestine nature of DELTA's mission, however, the full story of this extraordinary and sophisticated unit cannot be told no matter how important its unique capabilities are to the ongoing war against international terrorism. This relative anonymity makes DELTA an easy target for congressional budget cutters searching for a "quick fix" and the unit may well find itself as an expensive toy up for funding cuts in the austere future. Such actions would be disasterous.

The information in this book is based upon the research and experience of the authors and does not represent the positions or policies of any official, agency, or department of the United States government, British government, or any other government. The information was derived from unclassified publications and sources and is intended to neither confirm or deny, officially or unofficially, the views of those governments.

Uncredited photos in this book were taken by US armed forces personnel and are in the public domain. The names of current DELTA troopers are classified and, unless otherwise noted, all names given for soldiers below the rank of colonel are pseudonyms.

Chapter 1
Out of the Desert

The takeoff had to go right the first time. There would be no second chance. As the last item on the pre–flight list was checked off, the pilot revved up the EC-130E's Allison turboprops to gain maximum power. Releasing the already–straining brakes and pushing the throttles to the firewall, the pilot nursed his aircraft slowly forward out of the jumbled mass of wheel ruts furrowed deeply into the Iranian desert. The straining engines created a mini sandstorm that all but obliterated the ghastly funeral pyre they were leaving behind. Resembling some prehistoric bird of prey, the dark Hercules sluggishly lifted away from the makeshift desert runway and the disaster that Operation *Eagle Claw* had become.

This aircraft was one of the last special operations birds leaving Iran after the aborted rescue attempt to free American hostages in Teheran. The Ayatol-

lah Khomeini's Revolutionary Guards had held their fifty–three prisoners in the captured US Embassy compound for nearly six months and the half–dozen Hercules had been slated to play a key role in rescuing them. Now, as five heavily loaded aircraft flew into the early morning darkness, an EC-130E tanker and RH-53D Sea Stallion helicopter lay blazing in the desert. Through the swirling sand, passengers with portholes could clearly see what each had never believed possible: failure. Despite well–laid plans, the team's efforts had ended in an inferno of exploding ammunition and twisted, burning aircraft.

What happened at the refuel site code–named *Desert I* has been argued about and even embellished in a Hollywood adventure film, but the basic facts remain the same. The six special operations aircraft that penetrated Iran on the night of April 24–25, 1980 were configured either as tankers to refuel the Sea Stallion helicopters or as transports to bring in the assault teams and their ground support. After reaching the site, the mission was scrubbed

RH-53D Sea Stallions from the USS *Nimitz* practicing low–level formation flying before the attempted rescue of American hostages in Iran.

9

and the force had to prepare for exfiltration.

The decision to abort was made after three of the eight Sea Stallions either failed to reach *Desert I* or could not proceed because of mechanical difficulties. Not enough helicopters were available to carry out the mission, so there was nothing for the rotary and fixed–wing aircraft to do but return to their separate starting points. In preparation for the exfiltration, one of the RH-53Ds had to be repositioned. During that maneuver, the helicopter's main rotor smashed into the cockpit of a parked EC-130; both aircraft erupted into flame, and the explosions turned the stark desert night into a ghastly beacon. During the hasty evacuation of the site, the remaining Sea Stallions were left behind.

On board the EC-130E were members of America's newly formed counterterrorist unit known simply as DELTA. The unit had been activated in November 1977 but was untested or, as military professionals would say, "unblooded," and this was to be their first operational mission. But while the troopers anticipated that their baptism of fire would soon come in Teheran, they instead found themselves trapped in a terrifying inferno fed by thousands of gallons of aircraft fuel. As one of the survivors would later report, the DELTA Blue Team troopers and air crew from the stricken EC-130 struggled to "unass the muther" as best they could, bearing their injured with them.

Caught in the tanker's burning, smoke–filled cargo bay, Master Sergeant Leonard M. Harris was quickly overcome by smoke as he attempted to rescue an Air Force crewman. Luckily for both men, they were pulled from the burning plane by other

(**Top**) RH-53D Sea Stallions on the aft hangar bay of the USS *Nimitz* before launch and (**left**) a burned–out hulk at *Desert I*. Note the .50cal machine guns mounted in the cabin doors at the extreme left and right of the top photo. *Wide World Photos*.

members of DELTA.

Harris and the other survivors were loaded into various aircraft for the trip out. Now, as the last Hercules flew in a rough trail formation through the inky darkness toward the Indian Ocean and safety, Harris began to regain consciousness. Watery eyes fixed on a light on the cabin roof and then wandered down to scan the confusion around him in the crowded cargo bay. DELTA troopers, dressed in Levis, boots, and black field jackets, were interspersed with air crews, combat control team members, and other support personnel. Some sat in stunned silence, still wearing their woolen naval watch caps, while others were stripping off layers of body armor, web gear, and sweat–stained clothing. Checking his own physical condition, Harris was surprised that, despite his brush with death, the only damage that he was able to perceive, other than a raw throat from smoke inhalation, was a good singeing of his field jacket and a relatively minor burn across the back of his left hand.

Looking down at his recently black–dyed field jacket, he absently picked at the melted tape that covered the only insignia on the assault teams' tactical uniforms: a small American flag sewn on the right jacket sleeve. The troopers were to have displayed the flags after entering the Embassy grounds so that the hostages would readily follow them out during the exfiltration. After all, in their uniforms, the rescue team looked more like muggers in a New York subway than members of an elite counterterrorist unit.

Peering across the red–lighted cargo compartment, Harris realized that he and the rest of the passengers were sitting, lying, or in some other way trying to get comfortable while riding on the bouncing fuel bladder covering the length of the plane. While team medical personnel provided aid, others appeared to be sorting out what had happened to them. Regaining a sense of stability, Harris was

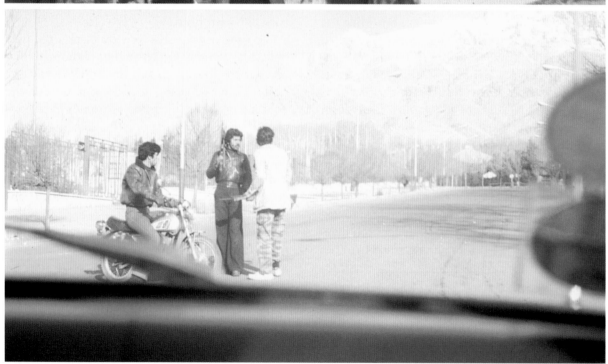

helped into a sitting position by another trooper. He noticed that his palms were wet with sweat, and not really knowing if it was from fear or just shock, he wiped them on his faded Levis. Leaning his head back against the cold metal skin of the Hercules, he muttered, "Good ol' Herky Bird." The vibration and steady hum of its engines made him think of his airborne instructors at Fort Benning, Georgia. "Damn if they weren't right," he thought. "The 130 *is* a living creature."

In the absence of the fear and pain that fatigue brings, he began to reflect on the events that brought him to this godforsaken situation. "How in the hell did I get in this mess?"

The Reception Committee

As the last of the special operations aircraft lifted off from the chaos of *Desert I*, another intense drama was taking place in the Iranian capital. From a clandestine communications site well outside Teheran, Dick Meadows, a highly decorated and skilled former Green Beret, received word of *Desert I*'s disaster. His vulnerable advance party of Special Forces soldiers had infiltrated the city only a few days earlier under various cover stories designed to hide all traces of their true identity and mission. Now, however, events beyond their control had forced them to immediately execute their own escape and evasion plans.

Nearly six months before *Eagle Claw*, on November 4, 1979, "subject matter experts" from all relevant military and civilian agencies were drawn to-

Revolutionary Guard checkpoints in Teheran surreptitiously photographed by Army personnel. They are armed with a variety of 7.62mm Heckler & Koch G3 rifles manufactured in Iran under a license obtained from the West German firm. (**Top**) A Revolutionary Guard is carrying several weapons to comrades up the street while, (**left**) the mountains ringing Teheran are clearly visible.

gether to form an ad hoc joint task force (JTF) charged with both the planning and execution of the hostage rescue. Like so often in the military, the "old boy" network was initially used to fill the JTF. This approach brought in many talented people whose broad range of expertise at first quickened the planning phase of the operation. Unfortunately, though, interservice and interdepartmental bickering soon created coordination problems. Despite later denials, virtually everyone either wanted a piece of the action or seemed intent on distancing themselves from the operation. The resulting problems—demonstrated by the initial lack of cooperation from the Central Intelligence Agency (CIA) and State Department officials—tended to frustrate rather than facilitate planning by the JTF's staff officers under the stewardship of Major General James B. Vought, a highly respected paratrooper who had much experience working with Rangers.

Ideally, CIA operatives would have already been in the "area of interest" providing current intelligence and would have been responsible for obtaining critical items such as "safe houses" and locally procured trucks in Teheran. However, at this time in its history, the agency was undergoing a number of reorganizations prompted by highly publicized criticism of its role in major incidents going back as far as the Bay of Pigs invasion of Cuba. Sensational reports of alleged assassination attempts on foreign leaders, Vietnam's numerous "black" or covert operations (including the unjustly maligned *Phoenix* program), and the increasing number of former CIA employees who turned into authors of "tell–all" books added to the growing public perception of a bumbling group of spies running amuck.

After Jimmy Carter assumed the presidency in 1977, he installed a fellow Annapolis graduate, Admiral Stansfield Turner, to oversee the restructuring of the CIA and the institution of his administration's "Georgia approach" to governmental man-

14

agement. Under Turner, hundreds of experienced personnel were laid off (referred to in the government's bureaucratic language as a reduction in force or RIF). The agency soon became heavily dependent on mechanical and technical means as the primary method of intelligence gathering instead of using them in conjunction with, or as a complement to, human intelligence collection, or HUMINT. By the time the Embassy in Teheran was seized, Middle Eastern operations were in a major decline; in fact, the last full–time operative in Iran had already slipped into the warm embrace of retirement.

Despite the CIA's reinfiltration of one of its agents into Teheran, DELTA's thirst for intelligence on a broad range of matters was not satisfied. The "black boxes" were clearly failing to produce the information required to carry out this delicate operation, and the *Eagle Claw* planners in DELTA began to look within the special operations community for HUMINT collection means to make up the shortfall. The search led them to Dick Meadows.

(Top) A mass demonstration at "Freedom Square" on Eisenhower Avenue about a half–dozen miles west of the US Embassy. In the unlikely event that Iranian mobs would react quickly enough to threaten the rescue mission, an orbiting AC-130H Specter gunship would perform "crowd control" around the embassy and prevent the armored vehicles based at an army ordnance depot to the north and the police headquarters near the Ministry of Foreign Affairs to the south from intervening. If the Specter found itself hard–pressed to keep the threats at bay, a second gunship covering Mehrabad International Airport to the west, would destroy Iranian F-4 Phantom jets, capable of chasing down the rescue aircraft, and assist at the embassy. (Left) A Revolutionary Guard bunker in central Teheran. The broad avenues which criss–crossed the capital, such as Roosevelt, which ran between the embassy and the soccer stadium and north to the army depot, were fed by an intricate—but well–mapped—maze of narrow streets fully or partially blocked by these randomly placed defensive positions.

This was not the first time that Meadows had participated in an effort to free US prisoners. Ten years before, he had been in charge of the compound assault team during Operation *Ivory Coast* (more commonly known as the Son Tay Raid), an airborne assault on a prisoner of war camp only twenty miles from Hanoi in North Vietnam.* Other exploits in Southeast Asia included the capture of North Vietnamese artillery pieces in Laos and the recapture of a major CIA outpost in that same country. He was an expert in what are referred to as "low–visibility insertions" and "takedowns."

Meadows had become a civilian advisor to DELTA after retiring from the Army, and his extensive background in clandestine cross–border operations, as well as his completion of the British Special Air Service (SAS) selection course, carried a great deal of weight in choosing him to enter Teheran ahead of the rescue force. Above all, the JTF planners knew he could be trusted to do his best to accomplish the mission—and, besides, he knew DELTA inside and out. This knowledge, however, could prove to be a rather negative aspect of his qualifications if he were caught.

Meadows' orders were to infiltrate the chaos of Teheran, establish a safe house, locally procure covered trucks to transport the rescue force, and guide the rescuers from the landing zone to their assault positions near the Embassy. In military terms, he was the reception committee and, on paper at least, this part of the operation was one of the less–complicated portions of the entire plan. One critical concern of Meadows was his cover and its associated background information and the story

---

*The over four dozen US prisoners were held at the camp but were moved shortly before the raid and remained in captivity until after the 1973 signing of the Paris Peace Accords. One side benefit of the operation, however, was an accidental attack on a nearby compound that apparently killed as many as 200 East Block or Soviet specialists involved in upgrading North Vietnam's air defenses.

A force of a dozen US Army Rangers and DELTA members made up two teams to secure the road running through the *Desert I* refuel sight. (**Above**) Troopers armed with a Colt M16 assault rifle and Walther MP-L submachine gun peer intently through the night. The relatively heavy PVS-5 night vision goggles, used during the operation, could only be worn for about thirty minutes at a time before a pilot or trooper would have to hand it off to a designated partner to wear. Within minutes after they rode their Yamaha motorcycles out of the belly of the first MC-130 to land, the team captured a bus with forty–four Iranian civilians, blew up a gasoline tanker truck with a light antitank weapon, and ran off another truck.

Although *Eagle Claw* planners were later criticized for establishing the refuel site in a moderately traveled area, mission parameters left them little choice, and DELTA planned to fly any Iranians taken into custody back to Misirah Island on the returning MC-130s. The Iranians would then be flown back to Iranian territory and released at Manzariyeh Air Base the following night. There were never any plans to hold any detained Iranians in exchange for the US hostages (such a move would have had disasterous political repercussions), and if the mission were aborted after they had been flown from *Desert I*, the Iranians would be speedily turned over to the International Red Cross for repatriation.

fabricated to explain what brought a Westerner to this hostile land. CIA liaison officers supplied him with an Irish background, including all the necessary documentation and accessories, while the JTF provided additional backups and an enhanced language capability in the form of three sergeants recruited in Germany, two from a covert Special Forces unit and one from the Air Force.

Unlike Meadows, these men already had covers and were conducting their daily lives under that blanket of anonymity. All were foreign–born nationals who had joined America's armed forces and were now US citizens. One of the men was a native of Germany and was intimately acquainted with the murky world of working with and supporting intelligence requirements levied on the Army by other agencies such as the CIA. Another of the operatives was born in the British Isles and was easily cloaked with the mantle of a Scottish background. The third (who had undergone no previous Special Forces training) was a native of the Middle East and was fluent in Farsi, the primary language of Iran. These men would provide Meadows with the additional skills required of the advance party.

When it was discovered, rather late in the planning, that three high–ranking hostages were being held in the Ministry of Foreign Affairs building six miles from the Embassy, an additional thirteen soldiers were recruited from a clandestine unit in Germany. Not enough time was available to change the basic plan as well as shift existing personnel to other targets, so it fell upon these men to fill the operational void created by the last–minute intelligence. Special Forces detachments like theirs had been preparing to fight potential Soviet invaders in the extensively built–up areas of western Germany since the late 1950s and were composed of experts in urban warfare.

Eagle Claw's mission profile called for the advance team to rendezvous with the DELTA rescue force staging out of a little–used airfield near Qena, 300 miles south of Cairo in central Egypt. Upon receipt of the execution message, the 132 men of the rescue force and additional support personnel flew on two C-141s from Egypt to an air base operated by British and Omani personnel on the large Arabian Sea island of Misirah. At the same time, the helicopter element located on the aircraft carrier USS *Nimitz* "patrolling" nearby in the Gulf of Oman prepared to launch its RH-53D helicopters to an isolated spot, code–named *Desert I*, in Iran's Dasht–e Karir (Salt Desert). While all this was taking place, a contingent of four AC-130E and H Specter gunships were readied for their launch the following night. They would fly directly from Qena to Teheran where they would support the rescue. The Specters would be refueled by KC-135 tankers as they passed over Saudi Arabia.

The next phase of the operation called for DELTA's surgical assault force, along with its security and support element, to take off from Misirah in EC- and MC-130Es of the 8th Special Operations Squadron. Their destination, *Desert I*, had already been surveyed by an Air Force Combat Control Team member who placed remotely operated infrared beacons along the "hasty" landing strip. After the force successfully rendezvoused at *Desert I* near Garmsar, 265 nautical miles southeast of Teheran, the assault element was to load onto the helicopters and fly on to *Desert II* in the rugged, mountainous region just southeast of the capital. Once there, the choppers would be hidden nearby, at a site codenamed *Figbar*, while the assault force linked up with the reception committee before dawn.

The assault force would settle in for the day while the DELTA commander, Colonel Charlie A. Beckwith would infiltrate Teheran along with a select group of twelve troopers who would receive the trucks gathered by Meadows' team near the city at a secure warehouse called the "Mushroom." It was their job to drive the small convoy out of the city on the second night of the operation and collect the rest of the rescue force from the hide site. After transferring to the six large, tarpaulin–covered Mercedes trucks and a Volkswagen van, 106 DELTA and Special Forces troopers would journey to the capital where final preparations for the impending rescue would be made. The plan called for the rescue force to depart from *Desert II* at 2030 hours and be in their designated assault positions by 2300 hours. Meadows would take Colonel Beckwith on a personal reconnaissance of the target before the attack at approximately the same time that the AC-130s were lifting off in Egypt.

The main assault group's three teams (code–named *Red*, *White*, and *Blue*) and Foreign Ministry assault group would use the principles of surprise, shock, and coordinated movement to take out the Ayatollah's Revolutionary Guards. As soon as the short, violent rescue operation erupted at the walled Embassy compound, the hidden RH-53D helicop-

(Top) An M151 roars over a a sand dune in Egypt. The soldiers given the mission of guarding the dirt road running through *Desert I* were not picked until after the main body of Rangers, slated to seize Manzariyeh Air Base, had arrived at Qena, Egypt. Intensive training was immediately begun for both the road-watch and airfield-seizure teams. **(Above)** Before operations could begin, Air Force ground personnel had to be flown into both Qena and the British-Omani air base on Misirah Island to set up communications and logistics for the thirty-four special operations tankers, transports, and gunships involved in *Eagle Claw*.

ters would emerge from their camouflaged position near *Desert II*. One would head for the large park surrounding the Foreign Ministry, while the rest would fly to sites at the rear of the Embassy compound and the Amjedeih soccer stadium across the

street, where both hostages and rescuers would be picked up. If the compound site couldn't be cleared of obstructions in time, all extractions would be conducted from the stadium.

Throughout the ground phase of the operation, one AC-130 gunship would orbit over the target area providing fire support, and another would cover the two Iranian F-4 Phantom jets on strip alert at Teheran's nearby Mehrabad International Airport. Two additional Specters would orbit close by in reserve. All parties concerned were fully confident that the massive firepower the Specters could bring to bear on the surrounding area would be more than enough to suppress any Revolutionary Guards attempting to reinforce their Embassy security force and prevent the infamous Iranian mobs from interfering with the rescue. As one of the gunship pilots was later to explain, the Specters' awesome firepower was the "best crowd-control measure" available.

While the AC-130s dominated the area, the helicopters would leave the chaos of Teheran for nearby Manzariyeh Air Base only thirty-five minutes away. Manzariyeh was to have already been secured by a seventy-five-man Ranger contingent and support personnel flying directly from Qena on four MC-130s. This elite light infantry unit was composed of experts in airfield seizure. Using M151s (commonly, if erroneously, referred to as jeeps) and commercial off-road motorcycles, they were capable of gobbling up the sprawling but lightly defended facility in a matter of minutes.

Throughout the exfiltration, F-14A Tomcat fighters and KA-6D Intruder tankers from the USS *Nimitz* would orbit over Persian Gulf waters—on call to knock down any hostile aircraft coming after the vulnerable transports, and gunships leaving Manzariyeh. If all went well, the entire force—Rangers, Special Forces, Meadows' team, support personnel, DELTA, and their newly rescued charges—would be quickly loaded aboard a pair of C-141s, which had made a quick dash from Dhahran, Saudi Arabia, and exfiltrate to Qena before the Iranians could take any effective countermeasures. There was no way to fly the helicopters out of Iran, and they were to be destroyed before the last Rangers left the airfield.

The catastrophe at *Desert I* changed all that. After Meadows received word over a clandestine radio to abort the mission, he notified the team, which dispersed from the safe house, and all made their individual ways to the passenger terminal at Teheran's Mehrabad International Airport. Security within the terminal was visibly increased. Unshaven and clad in an irregular mix of civilian and military clothing, the pride of Iran's Revolutionary Guard nervously paced back and forth near entrances, fingering their newly acquired Heckler & Koch G3 rifles. The menacing looks—as well as a healthy respect for the weapons' stopping power—caused Meadows to give each of the guards a grudging deference. Swallowing hard, Meadows entered the terminal entrance and walked directly to the Swiss Air ticket counter. Very deliberately, and somewhat slowly, he reached into the inner pocket of his corduroy jacket for the cash necessary to open the

Sea Stallions receiving preflight preparations on the deck of the USS *Nimitz*. The RH-53Ds had been freshly painted to mimic the look of Iranian helicopters and also carried green, white, and red Iranian identification roundels that could be added to further confuse prying eyes.

first of many doors to the waiting jet and freedom.

While being processed, he noticed that his "Scottish" comrade was in another part of the terminal area, being heavily questioned by a combination of Revolutionary Guards, customs officials, and men in soldiers' uniforms. Meadows later learned that the large amounts of US currency that had initially brought this unwanted attention to the Scotsman stayed in Iran with that "interested" group of officials. The newfound hatred of the "Great Satan" obviously did not extend into financial matters, and well–placed bribes of American greenbacks continued to do the trick.

Reaching down to retrieve his carryall, Meadows realized that despite the fact that word had been received about an "invasion" to the south, the security efforts within the airport remained disjointed and uncoordinated. Walking at a casual but determined gait toward the Swiss Air jet, he wondered what things were like at the Embassy.

Chapter 2
A New Game in Town

Kill one and terrorize a thousand.

Sun Tzu, 500 BC

Festering Arab resentment of America's direct and substantial support of Israel grew steadily after the United States became the Jewish state's chief sponsor in the wake of the 1967 Six Day War. By 1973, when massive American arms shipments played a critical role in blocking an Egyptian–Syrian victory in the Yom Kippur War, the United States was firmly planted on a collision course with the rising tide of pan–Arab nationalism. From now on, Americans would no longer be incidental victims of terrorist attacks. They would be the targets.

During the Six Day War, the sweeping successes of the Israeli military machine made it clear to the Arab world that change could not be guaranteed by conventional forces alone. One of the key audiences watching from the sidelines with a great deal of interest were the millions of Palestinians living in forced exile not only in the Middle Eastern countries, but also in Europe. Across the Atlantic, the United States was focused on the problems of the war in Vietnam, internal strife centered on the civil

One of the terrorists holding Israeli athletes at the Munich Olympics relays demands to German negotiators in front of millions of television viewers.

rights movement, and there was growing unrest on college campuses. Against this background, the United States hoped that every effort would be made to solve the numerous long–standing issues in the Middle East peacefully. Failing that, preventing disagreements from boiling up into open warfare was the least that could be strived for. But as world affairs would have it, the Palestinian issue exploded to the surface, amid smoke and gunfire, in the Hashemite kingdom of Jordan.

When shoved into a corner by Soviet–sponsored, Syrian–armed Palestinian forces intent on using his country as a staging area for raids on Israel, King Hussein ibn–Talal used his army to drive the Palestinians into Syria and reasserted his authority. The king and his Hashemite followers had never enjoyed an easy relationship with the various *fedayeen* groups making up Yasir Arafat's Palestine Liberation Organization (PLO), and its military arm, the *Fatah*, which was openly encroaching on the country's control of the Jordan River Valley. One faction, George Habbash's Popular Front for the Liberation of Palestine (PFLP)—the largest and most anti–Hashemite of the *fedayeen*—had worked feverishly to undermine Hussein's throne

21

Television crews and reporters line the balcony of the Beirut International Airport terminal during the nine–day hijacking of a TWA jet, June 22, 1985. The media was—and continues to be—one of international terrorism's most important weapons. *Wide World Photos*

long before the bloody confrontation.

The intense fighting for the capital of Amman and across northern Jordan in September 1970 caused a great deal of worry in the Western world, and supplies were sent in from a number of countries. Military forces were also alerted to move in and provide help, but the Jordanian Army succeeded without them. This stunning defeat of the *Fatah*–led Palestinians, however, laid the groundwork for the emergence of full–fledged terrorist organizations such as Black September, a radical group that operated as an arm of the "moderate" PLO until it split off on its own. The name itself commemorates the *fedayeen's* expulsion from Jor-

dan, and they took their revenge on the man who directed King Hussein's forces, Premier Wafsi Tal, by assassinating him the following year in Cairo.

While terrorists have never hesitated at murdering any Arab leader who was not in strict agreement with the dogma of their particular group, it is generally not considered socially acceptable to blame other "brother" Arabs for their numerous defeats to Israel. The fledgling terrorists saw the Western world as the cause of virtually all Arab problems—whether perceived or real—and several factors combined to make Western Europe an excellent target for their activities. Initially, these countries made particularly juicy targets because of their close proximity to the Middle East and the fact that their open societies allowed the terrorists a remarkable degree of freedom to carry out their activities.

These new terrorists were also a particularly media–savvy bunch who fully understood the ramifications of the still–evolving revolution in global telecommunications. Recent advances in television technology allowed the terrorist networks to increase their range beyond the printed word of newspapers, and much of the world's population now lived with their acts as a daily fact of life. Ratings–conscious news agencies and the viewers themselves had enabled the television camera to become one of the terrorists' chief weapons.

The use or threat of violence against individuals to affect a much larger, related group is not a new phenomenon; what is call "terrorism" today is a tactic of warfare that has been employed throughout history. Bombing, hijacking, assassination, and kidnapping are simply facets of this type of warfare magnified a thousand–fold by the electronic media. In the early 1970s, the world was introduced to such new television stars as Black September* and the Baader–Meinhoff Gang. Their activities were caught on television in 1970 when several commer-

The grand finale of the Palestine Liberation Organization's September 1970 hijacking of three civilian airliners. Their 300 passengers were held for a week and, after their release, the aircraft were blown up at an abandoned airfield near Amman, Jordan.

cial airliners were hijacked and taken with their 300 passengers and crew to Dawson Field, a desert airfield 40 miles from Amman that had formerly been used by Britain's Royal Air Force. After a week, the hostages were removed from the aircraft which were then blown up in full view of the world. But the event having the deepest and most far–reaching impact was the drama which unfolded at the 1972 Olympic Games in Munich, West Germany.

*One of the many organization names used by Sabri Khalil al–Banna (alias Abu Nidal) in an effort to sow confusion in the West as well as make the "armed struggle" against Israel appear larger than it is. In addition to Black September, other names used by the Abu Nidal Organization include: Fatah Revolutionary Council, Black June Organization, the Arab Revolutionary Brigades and Revolutionary Organization of Socialist Muslims.

Viewers were stunned by image after image of the wanton murder of innocents flashing across the screen, and governments in the West soon felt their power to control events slipping from their hands. Terrorist actions—or even the threat of such actions—were increasingly shaping policy decisions on major questions.

One ramification of these terrorist attacks not observed by the public was the new requirements

As an instructer looks on, a member of SAS takes position and returns fire against mock terrorists during a training exercise. He is positioned behind the engine block, which can provide adequate protection against most conventional pistol and rifle ammunition.

placed on international law enforcement and military forces. After the failure to negotiate or rescue successfully for the release of the Israeli athletes, West Germany's security needs were scrutinized from every possible angle with Teutonic efficiency. The findings were many, but the realists who would have to face the next round of fighting concluded that virtually every Western nation was now in the battle with this ancient form of warfare. The emergence of a new combatant—the counterterrorist—marked Western Europe's response.

Each country dealt with the new problem based on its own perception of how various political, economic, social, and, in some cases, religious factors af-

fected security considerations. The Germans established a special unit within its border police—later presented to the world as GSG-9, short for *Grenzschutzgruppe 9*—and the French formed the *Groupe d'Intervention de la Grendarmerie National* (GIGN). The British turned to their old standby, the SAS, while the Americans took the approach of wait and see, or more typically, "This will not happen to us." Yet, as the world continued to spin through the early 1970s, it was painfully obvious that the terrorists were moving a step or two ahead of the various national security forces and could attack whenever or wherever it was to their advantage. The organizations established to blunt terrorist attacks would, however, soon prove that they were forces to be reckoned with.

In October 1977 at Mogadishu Airport in Somalia, the German GSG-9 took revenge for their country's embarrassment at Munich by accomplishing a difficult aircraft "takedown" in response to a hijacking. Unknown to the terrorists, the Germans had learned much from the tragedy of Munich, and, with the help of two SAS commandos who blew open the aircraft's doors, a thirty-man GSG-9 force stormed the plane during the early morning hours. Later, in May 1980, the SAS gained international fame by conducting one of the most daring and highly publicized hostage rescues, when Pagoda Troop of B Squadron, 22nd SAS Regiment, launched their spectacular assault on the Iranian Embassy in Princess Gate, London, as television cameras broadcast the action around the world.

Preceding these events was the most famous rescue operation of the period: the raid on Entebbe Airport in Uganda, conducted by the Israeli special forces. Launched from bases within their own borders, more than 2,500 miles to the north, the commandos of Unit 269 flew directly into the site where 103 hostages were held. In the early morning darkness of July 4, 1976, Operation *Thunderbolt* was

Great Britain's 22nd SAS and US Special Forces have enjoyed a long, close relationship which began in earnest during the late 1950s. (**Above**) Lieutenant General Sir Charles Richardson, Britain's Director General of Military Training, inspects an SAS unit during an exercise with 5th and 7th Special Forces Groups at Camp Troy, North Carolina, September 28, 1962. General Richardson's visit turned out to be a pivotal event for the SAS. While the conservative British military establishment had grudgingly conceded the regiment's value in certain situations, the unit was generally thought of as little more than a "private army" of ill–disciplined mavericks that skimmed some of Britain's best soldiers from the top of traditional regiments. A tour with the SAS could kill a young officer's career.

At Camp Troy and Fort Bragg, Richardson witnessed SAS troopers studying advanced demolition and field medicine techniques plus engaging in specialized training in foreign languages, as well as a worldwide assortment of weapons. He left North Carolina greatly impressed with what he saw, and the almost immediate improvement in the attitude of the British military establishment toward the SAS was credited to the general's glowing report.

The same month that General Richardson visited SAS elements training in the United States, the US Special Forces soldier who would later found DELTA, Charlie Beckwith, was leading a troop from A Squadron, SAS, in a combined exercise with the French "paras" of the *1st Bataillon de Parachutistes de Choc* in Corsica. Beckwith had been attached to the regiment as part of an ongoing exchange program and, in 1963, would ship out to Malaya with the SAS to take part in deep–jungle penetration missions against guerrillas along the Thai border. The tour nearly cost him his life but, upon his return to Fort Bragg, he pushed hard (very hard) to have SAS training and organizational techniques adopted by Special Forces.

Israeli commandos, circa 1960, are representative of the high degree of individuality commonly found in elite special operations units. Informally dressed in a variety of military jackets, coats, scarves, and sweaters, they are a diverse lot with members who might easily pass themselves off as Britons, Arabs, Frenchmen, or Americans. Indeed, they may have once been Britons, Arabs, Frenchmen or Americans before emigrating to Israel. Such elite troopers from Unit 269 were responsible for the successful hostage rescue at Entebbe. Note the use of personal weapons of different types and calibers attuned to the taste of the individual soldier. The soldier in the center is armed with the standard Soviet assault rifle of the day, the 7.62mm Kalashnikov AK-47, while the others carry 9mm Uzi submachine guns, which were based on earlier Czechoslovakian weapons but designed and produced in Israel.

carried out with clockwork precision. Keeping it simple, the rescue force landed in four C-130s (why jump your men in when they can be landed in a nice neat package?). The lead Hercules casually taxied to within 200 yards of the terminal building holding the hostages, and a black Mercedes sedan— the standard mode of transportation of all Ugandan officers from company commander on up—rolled serenely down the ramp. The sedan cruised up to the brightly lit building, followed by a pair of nondescript Land Rovers, and suddenly disgorged nine Unit 269 commandos.

Within minutes, the Israeli strike force had secured the terminal area and airfield perimeter, removing a potential problem by blowing up the Ugandan MIG fighter aircraft and then loaded up the rescued hostages. The rescue force commander, Colonel Jonathan Netanyahu, was killed, as well as the entire terrorist gang and an undetermined number of Ugandan soldiers protecting the hostage takers. All but one of the hostages, an elderly woman who had been taken to a hospital and was later murdered, were quickly freed and flown to Nairobi, Kenya, where casualties were transfered to a waiting jet airliner equipped for medical emergencies. The GSG-9 chief, Colonel Ulrich Wegener, had also accompanied the Israelis, probably because two West German terrorists were involved in the hijacking.

Americans Become Targets

The United States entered the CT arena as a very unwilling participant. The primary reasons were America's deeply engrained tradition of keeping military and police powers well separated and the resultant conservative approach of the US military leadership when dealing with what they felt was inherently a police problem. Neither the political nor military hierarchies originally supported the view, held by many in the lower echelons, of the increasing danger to the United States and its interests by media–savvy terrorists.

US intelligence agencies gained their first direct lessons from the *nouveau* terrorists during the September 1970 uprising in Jordan. It was feared that *Fatah* insurgents would seize the US Embassy in Amman, and US paratroopers were alerted to, if necessary, seize the International Airport, allow an armored force to land, race into Amman and retake the Embassy.

As with Operation *Eagle Claw* some ten years later, the Jordanian rescue plan was complicated, unwieldy, and fraught with unnecessary risks. For example, the 509th Airborne Infantry, which was selected to seize the airport, would have had to fly to Jordan via an extremely lengthy, circuitous route from their staging area in West Germany. Instead of taking the normal route over continental Europe to reach the eastern Mediterranean, their operational plan called for a flight out into the North Sea and Atlantic Ocean around Spain to the Gibraltar slot, and then travel the length of the Mediterranean. The force would have to take this roundabout route because the "allies" of NATO would not grant overflight rights—a situation unpleasantly similar to what F-111 pilots would find sixteen years later during a retaliatory raid on Libya for sponsoring a terrorist bombing.

American planners were faced with a number of similar situations over the next two years, and missions were not approved for execution. Either White House or State Department jitters prevented the launching of airborne or Special Forces units to counter terrorist assaults. Terrorist networks in the Middle East, however, could easily strike soft targets and continued to target Israeli citizens. Americans stationed in Germany, as well as West Germans, found themselves the targets of former antiwar students now turned terrorists. In May 1972, the Baader–Meinhoff Gang, also known as the Red Army Faction, finally forced the issue on the United States by conducting six separate bombings.

Their targets were such sacred areas as the officers' club in Frankfurt and the headquarters building of US Army, Europe, located in the sleepy university town of Heidelberg. The news media provided some coverage of these strikes but, understandably, only a fraction of the blow–by–blow reporting which characterized the debacle of that year's Olympic Games.

While the taking of American hostages was not yet a problem, perceptive military leaders realized that the United States needed to be ready and able to respond to terrorism, and units within the Army's Special Forces community were tasked to conduct rescues using what is commonly referred to as the "hasty option response." In lay terms, this means that if the hostage takers begin to harm their prisoners, the team attempts a rescue as quickly and efficiently as possible. The lives of the hostages are of utmost concern, but the hasty response does not allow for the meticulous planning, coordination, and rehearsals that are required to carry out the surgical strikes so often associated with the highly skilled CT units. The hasty response is the operation that all counterterrorists hope they never have to conduct. It is the option that makes a commander wake up at night in a cold sweat.

Due to command relationship conflicts and the numerous constraints on personnel and funds, which prevent in–depth training, the hasty option mission is still found in a number of Army Special Forces groups around the world. This approach, however, leaves little for the in–depth training required to perfect even the most fundamental aspects of aircraft or room entry techniques.

Soon after Munich, a number of American military and civilian advisors recommended that a suitable force be established to fight terrorism. But it was not until the increased threat was brought home to President Jimmy Carter and the feasibility of creating a unit like those who struck at Entebbe

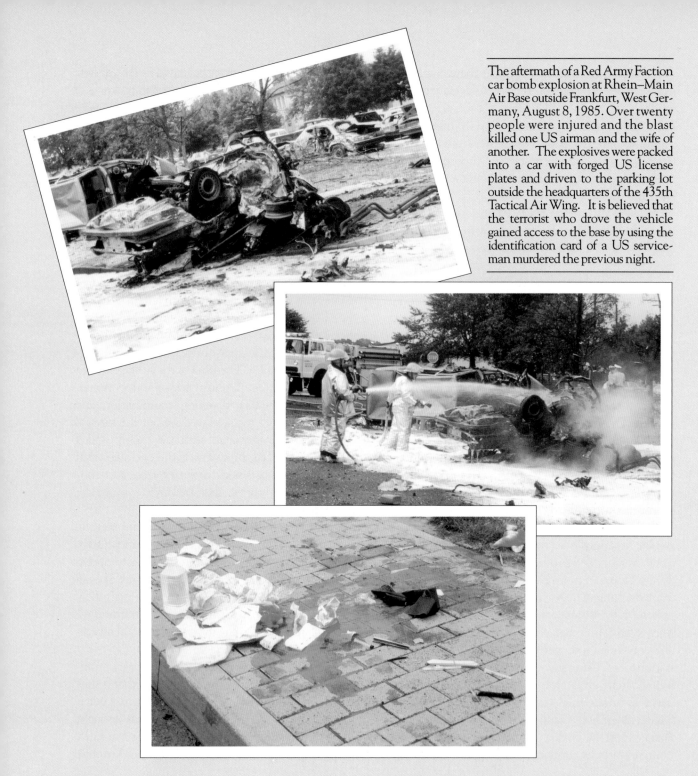

The aftermath of a Red Army Faction car bomb explosion at Rhein–Main Air Base outside Frankfurt, West Germany, August 8, 1985. Over twenty people were injured and the blast killed one US airman and the wife of another. The explosives were packed into a car with forged US license plates and driven to the parking lot outside the headquarters of the 435th Tactical Air Wing. It is believed that the terrorist who drove the vehicle gained access to the base by using the identification card of a US serviceman murdered the previous night.

and Mogadishu that the United States acknowledged the need to establish its own full–time, state–of–the–art counterterrorist response unit. The success of Operation *Thunderbolt* further confirmed the idea that many US planners had been fostering. The United States needed to have a small, surgical force capable of carrying out such operations. It was their contention that, despite the claims of the airborne community, Ranger companies and battalions were neither trained nor equipped for hostage rescues.

From the smoke of military infighting and political intrigue, 1st Special Forces Operational Detachment–DELTA was formed in 1977. Its name is derived from standard Special Forces terminology. Six ALPHA detachments (A teams), commanded by captains, make up a company–sized BRAVO detachment (B team), commanded by a major. A CHARLIE detachment (C team) is a battalion–sized organization commanded by a lieutenant colonel. Since the 1st Special Forces Operational Detachment was commanded by a full colonel and structured along completely separate lines, following the squadron–troop structure of Britain's famed SAS, it became a DELTA detachment. Using the concept of the troop and the squadron as the building block or base, it initially trained to conduct counterterrorist operations. Recent activities in Iraq and Kuwait, however, reveal that DELTA's one–dimensional media image of a super–secret counterterrorist team falls well short of reality. The 1st Special Forces Operational Detachment is a multifaceted unit much like its counterpart, the SAS.

DELTA and *Blue Light*

Both DELTA's sponsors and opponents within the military held firm—and diametrically opposed—ideas on who should respond to the terrorist challenge. The majority of DELTA's sponsors were typical of America's military leadership. They were extremely conservative officers who were slow to respond to the terrorist threat, but once convinced that it was very real indeed, they were bulldogs in their support of the unit. And, like its sponsors, those who had worked hard to undermine or sidetrack DELTA (primarily because they didn't understand the nature of the threat) eventually gave it their full support when ordered.

At the top was Army Chief of Staff General Bernard Rogers. This astute Kansan and Rhodes scholar watched as the armies of Great Britain and West Germany rapidly took on what most American policymakers refer to as "police powers" normally kept out of the military's hands. After the Carter White House made it clear that they wanted a unit with specialized capabilities, Rogers gave his blessing for DELTA's formation. He told the relevant senior planners that he wanted the unit operational—and wanted it now!

The individual most instrumental in DELTA's birthing process was Lieutenant General Edward C. "Shy" Meyer. As the Deputy Chief of Staff for Operations, he was one of the most influential senior officers on the Army staff. It was from his office, that plans and policy for how the US Army would operate were issued. General Meyer took a direct, personal interest in DELTA. From the time that the need for a counterterrorist force was identified through its birth and Operation *Eagle Claw*, Meyer was always present in some form, providing guidance and support. The rest of the Army may have called him "Shy," but to DELTA he was "Moses" because he always seemed to be able to part the waters for them.

Next in the line of supporters came General William DePuy, commander of the Training and Doctrine Command. General DePuy was *the* expert in training; even though he was as conventional a soldier as any, he clearly recognized that a force was needed "like the SAS," as he was often quoted as saying during major policy meetings. He had to be won over before General Rogers and others could be addressed, but that proved to be easy after his inquiries about similar organizations in Europe demonstrated that an effective CT unit could be formed within the US Army. He would provide the training support.

The remainder of the cast were found at Fort Bragg, North Carolina. Fort Bragg has often been referred to as "home of the airborne" because of the vast numbers of parachute and related units based there. Bragg was also the home turf of the members of the US Army's Special Forces. The individuals making up these organizations possess unique skills, and it was from this elite body that DELTA's supporters and opponents would come.

The architect of DELTA was the commandant of the Special Forces School: a gruff veteran of the guerilla wars in Southeast Asia named Colonel Charlie Beckwith. Not only did "Chargin' Charlie" have a wealth of experience in the realm of unconventional operations, but he also knew who the power brokers were and how to use them. For example, in 1975, when General "Iron Mike" Healy was reassigned from his command at the John F. Kennedy Special Warfare Center at Fort Bragg, his replacement was Major General Robert "Barbed Wire Bob" Kingston. Kingston's association with Beckwith could be traced back to the days when Beckwith was an exchange officer with the SAS and Kingston was with the British Parachute Regiment. The two had also just served together at the Joint Casualty Resolution Center in Nakhon Phanom, Thailand, in 1973–1974. Kingston would work closely with General Meyer to establish an SAS–type unit.

It was during Colonel Beckwith's tour as commandant that the special operations community watched Europe's response to the outrages of various extremist groups. Located in an area known as "Smoke Bomb Hill," members of the Special Forces refined their traditional skills and added the hasty response to their repertoire. Special Forces, however, were responsible for carrying out a wide range of missions and could not dedicate much of their training efforts toward hostage situations.

Other soldiers who lent their guidance and support during this critical period were the commander of the 10th Special Forces Group, Colonel Othan "Shali" Shalikashville; General Frederick J. "Fritz" Kroesen, of Forces Command, who controlled all units stationed in the United States; and the XVIII Airborne Corps's chief of staff, Brigadier General James Lindsay. At one point during DELTA's shaky beginning, Shalikashville lined up all his senior commissioned and noncommissioned officers and told them flatly, "The job that Colonel Beckwith has to do is more important than the job we have to do. I would encourage anyone who has the desire to try out for this unit." As for Lindsay, when General Kingston's successor refused Beckwith's request to move DELTA into Bragg's underutilized post stockade, he saw to it that the unit would get it, reasoning, "Here we've got a nice stockade facility where we're keeping eleven bad guys. . . . Why don't we take the eleven and put them downtown in the Fayetteville jail? Your use of the stockade is better than the use it's being put to now. Colonel, you've got it!" Beckwith was obviously pleased that his problem had been solved so quickly but believed that the general would never see another promotion because he was just too practical. Ten years later, however, Lindsay would wear a total of eight stars on his shoulders and become the commander of the newly created Special Operations Command responsible for providing combat–ready special operations forces for rapid deployment to other unified commands around the world.

Still, support of the special operations community was not very strong at this point. Meticulously trained Special Forces units had conducted numerous missions during the Vietnam War, but now there was not a need for such specialists—or so the conventional leadership thought. And the conventional leadership controlled the Army and downsizing in forces that was taking place. Providentially, control of Special Forces fell to the commander of the JFK Special Warfare Center, and since General Kingston, his boss, was in control, Beckwith had the degree of freedom required to bring DELTA on line.

Charlie A. Beckwith of DELTA, circa 1979.

Complaints by the Rangers that DELTA would deepen their current manpower problems (partially true) and that the unit duplicated some of their functions (untrue) were brushed aside early on. Beckwith's only real opposition came from the commander of the 5th Special Forces Group at Bragg, Colonel Robert "Black Gloves" Montell, who believed that the shoot–from–the–hip hasty response was perfectly adequate. Montell was one of the Army's most professional and experienced officers. Always impeccably dressed, he wore what was commonly referred to as the "Bad Tolz" uniform. With pistol belt stripped and worn over olive drab jungle fatigues, spit–shined jungle boots, and an ever–present pair of black gloves topped off by the coveted green beret, he provided even the most hard–eyed professional with a source of pride in those days after Vietnam.

About the time that the DELTA program seemed to be a sure thing, Kingston was transferred to Korea, and Major General Jack "Bobo" Mackmull assumed command. No doubt Mackmull had received his marching orders from Washington to keep the program on track, but as a West Pointer and aviator, he was not very familiar with the missions and capabilities of this strange little unit under his command and, unfortunately, made little effort to learn. Once DELTA was approved for activation, Mackmull was told to come up with a backfill unit until DELTA was certified for operations some two years in the future. Montell's 5th Special Forces Group received the nod.

To meet this requirement, Montell selected forty Special Forces troopers from within the community and trained them in hasty response techniques. This unit was code–named *Blue Light*. Operating under the principle that a bird in the hand is worth two in the bush, Mackmull threw his weight *Blue Light*'s way regarding both funding and personnel. Despite reassurances from insiders, it appears that Beckwith feared that Montell's stalwart professionals would derail DELTA before it had a chance to prove its concept. If Beckwith lost his support in Washington, he would lose his unit. And DELTA was truly his.

As with most endeavors, it is not necessarily who is the best qualified, but who has the most support. Initially, that is what kept DELTA and its concept of a full–time, low–visibility CT organization alive. When General Rogers discovered that expected resources were being routed away from DELTA, he, as they say, "went ballistic." From that point on, through the support from the chief of staff on down the line, DELTA was allowed to gain the necessary breathing room to grow from nothing to a full–fledged force.

After 1st Special Forces Operational Detachment–DELTA was activated in October 1977, Beckwith had to select and train his new unit. DELTA troopers would have to be able to blend perfectly into the civilian world, when required, and possess unique skills that included everything from the relevant military arts to climbing the sides of buildings and hot–wiring cars. As luck would have it, DELTA had just completed their certification exercises. The date was November 4, 1979.

A

B

C

D

E

F

Weapons and Equipment

Pistols

In the special operations community, an oft–repeated comment on the controversy over which round is better, the .45cal ACP (automatic Colt pistol) or the 9mm parabellum, goes like this: "Opinions are like assholes, everyone has one." Stopping power, mass versus velocity, number of rounds versus weight—the argument seems neverending but, over time, weapons firing the 9mm (.38cal) round have become respected additions to DELTA's arsenal.

Modern conventional warfare generally calls for relatively light–weight, high–velocity rounds such as the Colt M16's .223cal/5.56mm or NATO's standard .308cal/7.62mm, that are effective out to ranges of several hundred yards. For the takedown of a hostage holding site, however, 100 feet is considered an extreme range. What the counterterrorist needs is a heavy slug that will knock a man down with as few shots as possible, and rounds smaller than .45cal have often proven themselves to be inadequate against a determined enemy. As early as the beginning of this century, Moro warriors battling US soldiers in the Philippines were not stopped by government issue .38cal pistols and, most recently, in the GSG-9 operation against aircraft hijackers at Mogadishu, Somalia, the German commander was forced to empty his snub–nosed .38cal into a psyched–up terrorist who continued fight even as six bullets ripped into his body. For this reason, many operatives prefer to have a bigger weapon.

A big (*very* big) round like that from the Smith & Wesson .44cal Magnum will drop a hijacker in his tracks but, unfortunately, the high–powered bullet is likely to go through its intended target as well as several seats and passengers before it stops. Moreover, the .44 Magnum's substantial kick when firing can delay reacquisition of the same or other targets—possibly with disastrous results. The .45 ACP round fired by the Colt or Springfield Armory M1911A1 and other automatic pistols has a great advantage over its famous friend during takedowns. An old joke among shooters is that the .45's bullet travels so slowly that, for an instant, you can actually see it speeding towards the target. With such a low muzzle velocity—at roughly 830 feet per second, it's almost half that of the .44 Magnum— hostage safety is greatly increased since there is more likelihood that the captors' bodies will stop the bullets.

But while this would seem to make the .45 the obvious weapon of choice for takedowns, many shooters have gravitated to the 9mm Beretta Model

(**A**) The basic Colt 5.56mm M16A2 assault rifle, (**B**) Colt 9mm submachine gun, and (**C**) Colt 5.56mm Model 733 Commando assault rifle. (**D**) The Mossberg 12–gauge Cruiser 500 shotgun; (**E**) the Remington 7.62mm M40A1 sniping rifle mounting a ten–power US Marine Corps telescope instead of the Redfield twelve–power telescope commonly used by DELTA; and (**F**) the Spring-field Armory 7.65mm M21 sniping system based on the M14 rifle. (**G**) The Beretta 9mm Model 92F pistol, called the M9 by the US Army and (**H**) the Colt .45cal M1911A1 automatic pistol. (**I**) The General Motors Guide Lamp Division .45cal M3 submachine gun often described as "a pleasant gun to shoot"; (**J**) the Walther 9mm MP-K submachine gun, which served as a useful bridge between the M3 and (**K**) the Heckler & Koch 9mm MP5 submachine gun. (**L**) The Heckler & Koch 9mm MP5 SD3 submachine gun with integral silencer.

When DELTA was formed, its armorers developed special lighting equipment that could be attached to weapons for night operations. Today, such devices can be obtained off–the–shelf from manufacturers or are integral to the weapons. (Top) A Hensoldt aiming point projector fitted to a Heckler & Koch MP5 A2 submachine gun and (bottom, lower left) a laser pointer built into the forearm of a Mossberg 12–gauge shotgun. Also note the Stabo rings attached to the soldier's tactical vest and the flash/bang grenade (an SAS invention) ready for use in his left hand.

92 pistol. The high velocity of its 9mm parabellum slug is easily brought below 1,000 feet per second by reducing the round's charge, and, depending on which variant of the Model 92 is carried into a fight, the counterterrorist can count on making almost twice as many shots before reloading than he would if he carried a conventional .45cal automatic.

The automatic pistol made by Colt and the higher–quality product manufactured by the Springfield Armory, normally fire from eight– and seven–bullet magazines respectively, and can each carry an additional round in the chamber, while the Model 92 and its variants have thirteen– and fifteen–round magazines. The tradeoff is that while 9mm bullets are indeed smaller, their size is *adequate* and the Model 92 has more of them. Moreover, the ammunition a DELTA trooper carries on his body and in his weapon is all that he can count on having available to him during a takedown. If everything goes as planned, there will be very little shooting. If the operation "goes sour," its just DELTA and the terrorists in a high–intensity shootout of unknown duration. A situation can easily develop where the first side to run out of bullets loses and, with a weight nearly half that of a .45cal bullet, 9mm rounds can be carried in great quantity without encumbering a trooper.

Submachine Guns

The same holds true, of course, for submachine guns. Although pistols are preferred in most hostage situations, submachine guns become a necessity when large target areas or many terrorists (four and up) are involved. DELTA initially settled on the domestically produced .45cal M3A1 "grease gun," a World War II vintage weapon that went out of production in the early 1950s and was generally shunned by the US Army. Interestingly enough, though, the very features that made it unpopular with most soldiers, enabled it be an extraordinarily effective tool for room–clearing: a low muzzle velocity which allowed its heavy slugs to slam into—not through—a terrorist and a rate of fire slow enough to enable single shots to be squeezed off

The Heckler & Koch MP5 SD3 fires 9mm ammo and, with its collapsing stock and integral silencer, it is an outstanding weapon for the closein fight. The sound supressor is a two–stage external silencer. The first stage of the system will absorb gasses while the second absorbs the muzzle blast and flame. The bolt noise is absorbed by buffers made of rubber. If you use subsonic ammo, the report cannot be heard more than fifteen to twenty feet away.

without disturbing the shooter's aim.

Acquiring adequate replacement parts for the weapon was an armorer's nightmare, however, and the old friend soon made way for a variety of submachine guns. Selection of weapons is a personal choice that often revolves around such factors as weight, reliability, how often must you clean it between firings, amount of ammo per magazine, and accuracy after it has been beat up in a parachute jump. The Heckler & Koch MP5 and the less expensive, easily concealable Walther MP-K are both German arms that fire 9mm rounds, as does the Colt submachine gun that has many parts common to the M16 rifle. The compact Colt Model 733 Commando assault rifle also benefits from this commonality and can be used on missions requiring its higher velocity 5.56mm round.

35

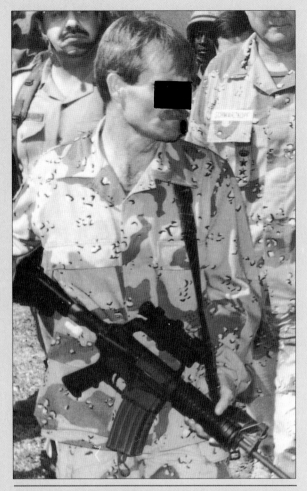

Trooper in southeastern Iraq armed with a Colt Model 727 carbine. Note the troopers sterile uniform (no identification or other markings) and longish hair. A three-power telescopic site is mounted on the carbine.

Shotguns

Shotguns are also useful in a variety of situations but are most commonly associated with forced entry techniques. Heavy rifled slugs can be depended on to supply the pure smashing power needed to quickly and efficiently blow the hinges off most doors. Sabot rounds, on the other hand, allow deeper penetration of the target and are best employed against vehicle or aircraft engines and door-locking mechanisms. After initial entry has been gained at a hostage holding site, shotguns can be used to force additional doors or, if necessary, against the hostage takers.

A 12-gauge rifled slug (**left**) and 12-gauge sabot slug (**right**).

Ammunition

Terrorists cannot be reasoned with and will attempt to kill their captives if a rescue is attempted, so when choosing ammunition, CT specialists want a man stopper that will knock a terrorist down and keep him down. While the heavy .45cal remains an ideal round for hostage situations, the lethality of smaller slugs, like the 9mm, can be greatly enhanced by using "soft-point" bullets with hollow or flat tips. The unusual point causes the soft, lead slug to expand into a broad, mushroom-shaped projectile upon entering the body, often doubling in diameter and increasing its shock effect dramatically. In a war where the armed forces of one nation are openly pit-

(**Left** to **right**) Flat-point, hollow-point and conventional bullets.

ted against those of another, the rules of land warfare prohibit the use of such ammunition. DELTA troopers participating in a hostage rescue, however, are not subject to the restrictions of the Geneva Convention. Like their police counterparts, they can legally use hollow-point ammunition (or exploding rounds that shatter on impact) to subdue captors and save the lives of the hostages.

The actual weapons and ammunition used on a mission are determined by the nature of the target.

A takedown of an oil platform, for example, is a very different affair from that of an airliner cabin crowded with hostages sitting upright. Only the team members assaulting areas likely to contain the platform's captive crew need to worry about carrying weapons with limited velocity.

Advances in technology have also complicated matters for DELTA and other CT specialists by adding dangerous factors to the equation such as handguns and bombs with almost no metal parts. Initially, only law enforcement agencies and the military had access to the lightweight body armor made from Kevlar fabric (which, incidentally, does *not* set off metal detectors). Over the passage of time, however, this type of highly effective armor has greatly proliferated and, if not already in terrorist hands, can be easily obtained by third parties or simply stolen. When worn in thin, easily concealable layers, Kevlar will stop the low–velocity slugs normally required for passenger safety. Technology and tactics have provided solutions to these and other problems but the decades–old argument over the most appropriate weapons to use is something that will die harder than any flesh–and–blood fanatic.

Sniper Rifles

Nearly all DELTA weapons—whether old or new—have been "accurized" to some degree by the unit's own gunsmiths. Loose–fitting parts typically found even in quality mass–produced weapons are replaced by custom–built pieces with closer tolerances, specialized trigger mechanisms, and better sights. For example, before it was superseded by the heavy–barrelled 40XB sniper rifle (which was specially manufactured for DELTA by Remington Arms), modifications were made to the trusty old M14A1 to upgrade its already formidable performance as a sniper rifle.

Modifications typically included polishing and hand fitting of the gas cylinder and piston to im-

prove operation and reduce carbon buildup. Barrels were always carefully selected to ensure correct specification tolerances and are bedded into the forearms with a fiberglass compounds. Trigger housing groups were carefully fitted and polished to provide a crisp hammer release and suppressors fitted to eliminate sound and flash which could give the sniper's position away. Receivers could also be individually fitted to stocks using a fiberglass compound. The US Army now purchases an off–the–shelf versions of this weapon from the Springfield Armory called the M21 sniping rifle. DELTA troopers often use this weapon during training and it also receives considerable reworking such as having plastic spacers added to customize the length of the stock. The M40A1 and M24 sniping systems,

Flash/bang grenades with no–snag caps in an Eagle Industries hip pouch. Center pockets hold thirty–round clips for 9mm Heckeler & Koch submachine guns.

Nomex balaclava

Goggles with shatterproof lenses

H & K 9mm MP5 A2 submachine gun

Eagle Industries Tac III assault vest

Kevlar vest

Flex cuff pouch

Nomex gloves

Spare thirty–round magazine clipped to engaged magazine

Gas mask pouch

Flashlight pouch

Gadget bags

Additional 9mm pistol magazines

Rappelling belt

Beretta 9mm pistol with extended magazine

Additional 9mm submachine gun magazines

Spare 9mm magazine

Flash/bang grenades with no–snag caps

Nomex coveralls

Eagle Industries flash/bang pouch

Assault boots

DELTA troopers (and all CT specialists) wear mission–specific gear. For example, while the man at left is equipped for an "average" take-down, the SAS trooper at right is set to operate in a chemical environ-ment and wears the minimum possible gear around his chest and hips to help ensure that nothing will snag his climbing rope.

standardized versions of the 40XB, are also being acquired by the Army and Marine Corps.

Grenades

The famous "pineapple," more properly known as the Mk II fragmentation hand grenade, is what most people think of when this type of weapon is men-tioned, but the long–obsolete pineapple was pulled from front–line service with the US Army over a decade before DELTA was formed. A cylindrical canister, about the size of a shaving cream can, is used for concussion grenades, chemical grenades (such as tear gas), and the flash/bang grenade (a description of the grenade's employment is on page

57). This design allows the grenade's user to gently role it a predictable direction and distance into a room, unlike the Mk II and its similarly shaped or round descendants which are designed for throwing and, if rolled, could wobble almost anywhere—including back up against the very wall that a troop-er is using for shelter! Before the recent fielding of the flat–sided M560 series fragmentation grenades, if a mission profile called for use of an antipersonnel grenade with a predictable roll, an M57 or M61 would have to be soldered into an appropriately sized tin can to achieve the desired effect. Once the pin was pulled and the safety lever fell away, a nearly perfect roll could be achieved every time.

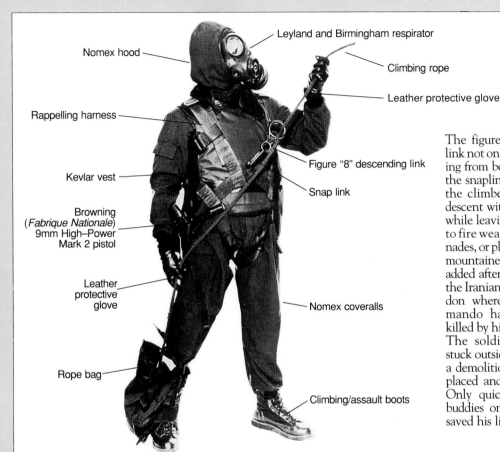

Nomex hood

Leyland and Birmingham respirator

Climbing rope

Leather protective glove

Rappelling harness

Figure "8" descending link

Snap link

Kevlar vest

Browning
(*Fabrique Nationale*)
9mm High–Power
Mark 2 pistol

Leather
protective
glove

Nomex coveralls

Rope bag

Climbing/assault boots

The figure "8" descending link not only prevents clothing from being dragged into the snaplink but also allows the climber to control his descent with only one hand while leaving the other free to fire weapons, throw grenades, or place charges. This mountaineering device was added after the operation at the Iranian Embassy in London where an SAS commando had almost been killed by his own explosives. The soldier had become stuck outside a window after a demolition had been emplaced and its fuse ignited. Only quick action by his buddies on the roof above saved his life.

Clothing

From the early days of hasty option operations, counterterrorist equipment has steadily evolved. Lightweight, highly rigid specialized clothing and equipment has now become a standard for CT teams. Several European units such as the SAS and Germany's GSG-9 found out through practical experiences at the Iranian Embassy in London and at the Mogadishu airport that general issue equipment is great for conventional forces but suffers from dangerous shortfalls when used during specialized operations. Much of the evolution in equipment has focused on the tactical assault vest and modular pouches attached to the upper torso and hips.

They incorporate such items as extra ammo, radio, and first aid pouches along with rappelling rings. Counterterrorist operations are very personal affairs. Despite the fact that the soldiers belong to teams, each man puts a great deal of faith in his individual gear. The equipment *must* be capable of accommodating number of modifications to handle, for example either flash/bang or gas grenades; MP5 magazines or Colt 733 Commando magazines. The problem was solved by creating a basic vest capable of handling interchangeable sets of pouches and holders for the problems specific to a given mission.

Chapter 3

The Making of a DELTA Trooper

In the 82d Airborne, I was better than any guy in my company. Over here I gotta hustle just to keep up.

a DELTA trooper

Joining a counterterrorist unit is very similar to breaking into the big leagues of pro sports. There are a few differences, however. Major league ball clubs have quite a few rookies on the squad, whereas the CT arena requires that units be composed exclusively of veterans with basic special operations skills already refined to a razor edge. And an error in the major leagues won't cost you your life or the lives of your team members.

CT units are composed of senior noncommissioned officers (NCOs) and several rather well–qualified officers. Continuous assignments in such units have not always been career enhancing, and despite the Army's recent elevation of Special Forces to full branch status, few officers stay around for more than one or two tours with the Special Forces groups. Those who do are usually *extremely* dedicated to their units, its troops, and the basic

US and German counterterrorists conducting a joint exercise involving rappelling, door–busting, and room–clearing techniques.

idea that the worldwide terrorist threat and its network of supporters should be met head–on and eliminated. They usually hold the respect of their fellow team members, who are not as concerned with an officer's rank as they are with his ability to shoot straight and back up his team.

Counterterrorism is only one of the missions assigned by law to the special operations community. The men who are charged with carrying out these low–visibility operations are chosen from a wide range of backgrounds and spheres of our society. Each is selected based on his talents and the unit's need to fill particular slots within its ranks. The question, "How does the whole process start?" begins with this fundamental requirement to fill open positions.

Selection and Training

Special operations units, and especially the close–knit counterterrorist outfits, recruit in several different ways. Special attention is given to the "old' boy network." As with any other business or

All DELTA trainees are jump qualified, and previously acquired skills, such as scuba diving are further refined during training. Troopers are assigned to specialized teams containing soldiers with the same skills. Many teams and elements are multidisciplined.

occupation, word of mouth and vouching for someone are key ingredients in the selection process. A second method is to simply advertise the need for people. DELTA recruitment teams make the rounds of training centers, troop posts, and such facilities as the Command and General Staff College or NCO advance schools. These recruitment drives preceed DELTA's fall and spring selection and assessment courses. Recruitment letters are also routinely mailed from Army personnel centers and, more recently, as the unit has edged out of the black into a rather dark grey, volunteers have been openly solicited in Army journals.

DELTA's rigid entrance requirements are clearly spelled out for career officers and NCOs who may be enticed to leave behind the warm comforts of their current postings for a new adventure. The pitch is always straightforward and unambiguous:

"ASSIGNMENT OPPORTUNITIES are available in the 1st Special Forces Operational Detach-

ment–DELTA. DELTA is the Army's special operations unit that has been organized to conduct missions that combine rapid response with the surgical application of a wide variety of unique skills and the flexibility to maintain the lowest possible profile of US involvement. . . . DELTA gives commissioned and noncommissioned officers unique opportunities for professional development. . . ."

A fourth and less–known method is for soldiers to be individually sought out by recruiters, based on a screening of their official records. This method may also be used with word–of–mouth recommendations. Recruiters are usually looking for specific assets, such as language skills, key past assignments, military qualifications, or schools attended. From the compiled list of likely candidates, individuals are contacted and asked to volunteer.

Drawn from the Active Army, Army Reserve, and Army National Guard, all DELTA members must pass a background security investigation, be at least twenty–two years old, male, and a US citizen. Each soldier's records are screened for psychological abnormalities or recurring discipline problems, and those accepting the challenge receive very thorough physical and eye examinations. Commonly referred to as the Scuba/HALO physical, it is akin to the in–depth exams pilots receive.

After getting the thumbs up from the doctors, or "chancre mechanics," the prospective counterterrorist is subjected to a battery of tests to determine if he is psychologically sound. The last thing a unit in the midst of a mission needs is to find itself saddled with a would–be Rambo or a real–life psycho. The cost of not conducting extensive psychological tests was graphically displayed as early as the Munich incident in 1972. At one point, the terrorists moved into the sights of the German sharpshooters who then froze. The results were quite unsatisfactory from the Israelis' standpoint.

Approximately 100 prospective counterterrorists receive intensive physical testing every session and high scores are an absolute requirement. In DELTA's formative stage, its selection process closely followed the British SAS model. This was due to the fact that many of the individuals who had a hand in setting up the unit were the products of SAS–Special Forces exchange programs and the close working relations these units have always had. This aspect of the month–long selection process has not changed.

The candidate's ordeal begins with six grueling events which must be completed within a designated period and earning a minimum of sixty points each. The candidates are, of course, expected to do better than the minimum. Periodically, small modifications are made to the test; examples of what is expected of the volunteers include: forty–yard inverted crawl in twenty–five seconds; thirty–seven situps in one minute; thirty–three pushups in one minute; run, dodge and jump course in twenty–four seconds; two–mile run in sixteen minutes, thirty seconds; and 100–meter swim while fully clothed and wearing boots.

Following the test, the candidate has the opportunity to show how well he can accomplish a speed march. The route covers eighteen miles, and the

Soldiers using the Stabo technique to land on a Fort Bragg rooftop. Hanging free from the helo during their approach, the men land simultaneously instead of one at a time. The target area is framed with a two–by–four barrier in case any of the soldiers loses his footing.

individuals must traverse it as rapidly as possible. Since this is one of the psychological problems to overcome, the passing times are never published. However, most of those who have passed it seem to agree that ten–minute miles are almost too slow!

Those who have made it this far into the selection process now receive a real treat. Just like in the SAS course, the candidates now are asked to really show what they are made of and are taken to one of several sites for a combination speed march, compass course, and survival exercise. Tests were originally conducted near Troy, North Carolina, in the Uwharrie National Forest, but are now done on the even more rugged terrain of Camp Dawson, West Virginia; recently, a test site has been added in the secured areas of Nellis Air Force Base, Nevada.

The Freedom to Fail or Succeed

If you were one of the few candidates to reach the forty–mile land navigation exercise, you'd find that the basic scenario goes like this: With all the ceremony of going off to a maximum–security prison, you and the other candidates are trucked out to the test site, where each is dropped at separate starting points. As dawn begins to break, you are given a set of instructions that amount to little more than a compass heading and a point on the map marking the final destination perhaps a half–dozen miles away. You are to pick out your route, keeping in mind that the object is to get there as quickly as possible.

Off you go. As soon as you leave the gentleman who gave you the instructions, your thoughts run the gamut of, "What the hell am I doing here?" to "I hope I can pull this off." Even though you made some rough calculations at the starting point, you drop off to the side of the trail to double check the situation and ensure your initial calculations are correct. (Besides, you didn't want to look indeci-sive in front of the guy at the drop–off point.) Squinting more closely at the map, you find that the contour lines are so close together that they look like some gigantic drunk worm. In other words, it is all up and down, with a few nice cold creeks in between. Off again, you settle into the comfortable trot the old hands taught you back at Bragg's Smoke Bomb Hill or Fort Benning. As usual, it starts to rain a little, but for the average Airborne, Ranger, or Special Forces type, rain is not a stranger. Checking your compass to keep oriented, you now settle into the routine. In most cases, the trial would be more enjoyable if you didn't remember that this was much more than just an exercise. You are here to show someone that you can hack whatever it takes to be part of that group called DELTA.

As you navigate along the trail, the shoulder straps of your fifty–five–pound rucksack begin to make themselves known to you—especially as the ruck gets wetter. Sweat trickles down your armpits, gets in your eyes, and seems to find refuge in your already chaffed crotch. After about the first hour and a half, the experience factors of Ranger School and the Special Forces qualification course, along with the numerous Special Forces Group exercises, take over. So it's time to stop, take stock of the situation, and drink some water. Pausing along the trail, you look around the dense hardwoods that make up much of the terrain along the mountains. Sensing something in the underbrush near your left jungle boot, you slowly retreat a few steps as "Jake no shoulders" decides to rattle a friendly greeting. Your mind comprehends the danger, but in some ways you really do not want to think about what could have happened, especially if he got upset as you were sitting down to check your feet.

Moving down the trail, you find a better place to get out of the drizzle and change your socks and apply some Vaseline to your sensitive areas. You get your bearings one more time and are off. Whether you are running the selection course in the mountains of Appalachia, with its forests and numerous streams, or driving on in the Sierra Nevada wastelands, the expected results are the same. Just like General Forest, get there "firstest with the mostest." In your case, get there fastest—period.

You've been at this all day, the sun dipped below the wooded hills uncounted hours ago, and at each rendezvous, you hope that it will be the one site where you will be told to throw your ruck into the truck and get aboard. But for some bizarre reason, the only words you hear at each brief stop are the location of your next rendezvous. After about a dozen hours of this, many volunteers begin to rest too long or slow down so much that they are unable to make the twenty–hour time limit. Even good soldiers begin to look for excuses to quit, and many inevitably find them. But not you. Cold, wet, and numb with exhaustion, you move off again, continuing in search of whatever you are out here for until well after midnight, when you are unceremoniously informed that the exercise is over. The survivors rarely remember exactly where they've been and, as with the speed march, even know how far they went or how long it took.

By now, the steady attrition of volunteers has weeded the field down to perhaps a dozen or so survivors. Many of those returning to their home units have been cut because they were unable to

An exhausted instructor from the John F. Kennedy Special Warfare Center training group, after negotiating a demanding confidence course like DELTA's. He is indicative of the highly motivated, professional soldiers in the US special operations community.

meet the tough physical and navigational challenges, while others were sidetracked for other legitimate reasons, such as knee, ankle, or back injuries. Some, however, drop out because they simply were not mentally prepared to follow the course through to the end without the accustomed "you can do it!" prodding that had been an integral part of all previous training. The NCOs overseeing the selection course steadfastly refuse to provide this encouragement. In any event, DELTA makes a great effort to ensure that those not selected know that they are

A trainee negotiates stairsteps to a room mock–up during entry technique training at the SOT. The object is to engage the pop–up silhouette targets from uncomfortable angles while in motion.

not failures. Each candidate receives a certificate of training and is simply told he was not selected.

Looking back at the physical side of the selection process, a key aspect becomes crystal clear: It is structured to put the maximum psychological pressure on those being tested. The individual is provided the freedom to succeed or fail on his own. A candidate not only must know his physical, mental, and emotional makeup, but must be able to use it to his advantage. In the CT arena, there are many occasions where individual actions are required, and in those life–and–death situations, you get only one chance to succeed. As Sun Tzu pointed out

so long ago, you have to know yourself as well as your enemy. If you are not ready to run in seemingly aimless directions for hours through the dark, wet, torturous terrain of overgrown, forested mountains, the cross–country land navigation exercise is not for you. If you are not ready to know what real fear is, to meet it head on and beat it, DELTA is not for you.

The trip back to Fort Bragg takes on an unreal atmosphere after what has occurred. Every selection course will have a variable number of thoroughly exhausted candidates who will go on to face the final and, according to some, hardest part of the selection process: the interview. A board of DELTA veterans grills the survivors and determines who goes on for training.

"So you're infiltrating an unfriendly area prior to taking down a terrorist hideout. Say you come across two little girls. You can't leave them. Do you take them along, tie them up, or do you kill them?"

"Tell us a little about Machiavelli."

"What were the arguments for and against our acquiring the Virgin Islands during World War I?"

"Was President Truman right or wrong to fire MacArthur?"

By this point in the four–hour grilling, some volunteers have taken on the look of frightened animals. The questions are asked seriously, and the DELTA veterans expect serious answers.

"Well, Sergeant, you've given a fine performance so far. Now tell us what you tend to blow it on."

"Why should we take you? What can you offer DELTA?"

"You're a good soldier!? So what!? Sergeant, we're up to our ears in good soldiers. Tell us about your unique skills, what you're really good at that's not military related."

In this tension–charged atmosphere, there are few right or wrong answers. The board is looking at the individual as a whole: his values and how he is able to handle himself in this situation.

The objective of the selection course is to find individuals who can both work with the team and yet operate independently without orders. In the end, only about ten percent or fewer of the initial candidates actually make it into DELTA; and a rumor circulating through the special operations community contends that one group moving throughout the selection process lost virtually every man before the assessment was finished. While such an occurrence could certainly wreak havoc with the manning levels of a small, highly special-ized organization, such problems can be ironed out if they are not persistent. Moreover, the nature of DELTA necessitates that its emphasis must remain focused on the quality, not quantity, of personnel entering the unit.

The SOT

As the new DELTA trainee drives along Gruber Road past MacKeller's Lodge, he thinks back to the recent events of the selection course. Now the staff sergeant is at Fort Bragg, reporting in for some of the finest—and toughest—training in the world. To his right, he sees a high cyclone fence and dirt road used by the security force who patrols it. Beyond the fence and nestled within the rough horseshoe formed by Gruber, Lambert, and Manchester Roads is the secure training facility constructed for the training of America's elite CT units and the home of DELTA. Called the Special Operations Training Facility (SOT), the multimillion–dollar complex became a reality through the increased support from congress and the president for the war on terrorism in the early 1980s.

Almost as if the world has opened up its secrets, the SOT unfolds in the form of large two– and three–story buildings and training areas for heli-borne insertions. The staff sergeant is immediately struck by how easy it is for virtually anyone to get a look at this surprisingly well–publicized facility. With counterterrorism such a security–conscious business, this visual access seems odd, but he writes it off as the price DELTA must pay for being on an "open post" like Fort Bragg and chuckles to himself when he remembers what started the whole process that led him to Gruber Road today: a public an-nouncement in his branch journal, *Infantry*, that "assignment opportunities" were available in DELTA.

The newcomer passes the SOT's entrance and continues to drive north toward Manchester Road. He is rewarded with a clear view of numerous open–aired and enclosed ranges he'll be seeing a lot of over the next two years. A thrill rushes through him. This is going to be the ultimate adventure! Coming back to the reality of the moment, he makes an un-authorized U turn and pulls up to the brick guard-house at the gate. His identification is scrutinized

A trainee practices pistol shooting at multiple targets at one of the SOT facility's numerous ranges. Note the semi–crouch stance and two–handed pistol grip.

against the incoming roster for the day, and he is directed to park and await his escort. The games, as they said in ancient Rome, are about to begin.

So far, everything the trainee has seen speaks well of the command emphasis placed on the Army's counterterrorist mission, from the White House down through the major subordinate headquarters, the Joint Special Operations Command (JSOC). In military terminology, it is a "high–speed" operation. As DELTA's newest recruit waits for his escort, he is startled to see an MH-6, bristling with darkened human figures instead of gun pods, zoom overhead. Along each side is a trio of soldiers buckled into special side platforms for rapid egress. Unseen by the trainee, the six commandos slip wearily from their "Little Bird" just a moment later at a helicopter pad near Lambert Road.

This specially modified Hughes chopper belongs to another important part of the team, the 160th Special Operations Aviation Regiment (Airborne), or SOAR. This unit is a result of the many problems experienced during *Desert I* and objectively outlined in its after–action review. Commonly referred to as the Holloway Report, it pointed out that a major area to restructure, if future missions were to stand a chance, was helicopter operations, and the covert aviation unit was duly formed at Fort Campbell, Kentucky. Originally named Task Force 160, it soon became the major US Army aviation support element for DELTA.

The commandos clearing the aircraft have darkened faces and wear a patrol, or "Ranger," cap. Clad in sturdy, olive drab jungle fatigues plus a wide assortment of specially made vests and other web gear, they also carry rappelling gloves, snaplinks and nonstandard Heckler & Koch MP5 submachine guns. As the SOAR 160 bird rises back into the sky, its stubby, rounded frame gives it the appear-

American counterterrorist team practicing pistol shooting from several different positions. Ranges such as this one provide enclosed areas to practice room–clearing methods out of sight of prying eyes.

ance of an overweight bumblebee or lethargic beetle attempting to gain flight.

Most CT operations require lightning fast entrances into the target area, along with shock effect and disorientation of the hostage takers. Carrying out such complicated maneuvers requires a great deal of training, teamwork, and the building of mutual respect for each member's abilities. That is what the new recruits are to learn during DELTA's five–month operators course at the SOT.

The facility's mission is to teach new methods and refine old skills in the art of counterterrorism. Many writers and observers have referred to the skills of eliminating a terrorist situation as antiterrorism. This, however, is incorrect. Antiterrorism is a term that refers to skills and techniques used by people or organizations which will help *prevent* them from becoming the victim of a terrorist attack. There are schools and courses where basic antiterrorist methods and tactics are taught, but the SOT addresses the final options of dealing with a terrorist incident that has *already occurred*. This is where DELTA comes into play: the counterterrorist arena.

Whenever the complex subject of counterterrorism is raised for discussion or debate, the argument that a specialized unit for CT operations is too expensive in terms of manpower and money usually comes to the fore. Regardless of whether this view is correct, it is undeniable that the political impact of a successful terrorist attack is often immense; the economic costs alone can run into the tens of millions of dollars, and priceless, innocent lives are put at risk or even lost. That is why dedicated units tasked to conduct CT operations are a must. How such units are configured is the decision of each country that fields them. Yet, one piece of the equation remains firm: Counterterrorist skills are highly perishable and must be kept at razor's edge if the team hopes to succeed. Appropriate training and constant studying of the enemy's methods, personnel, and organizational structure are an absolute necessity. The required skills and support apparatus are manpower– and resource–consuming, but countries employing counterterrorist units must be prepared to accept the costs. In the long run, it is a low–budget affair when compared to the economic and human costs of a successful terrorist strike.

A CT operation is composed of several distinct phases. First, the unit must get to the area of operations— possibly many hundreds or even thousands of miles away— by reliable, secure transportation. Simultaneously, immense amounts of intelligence must be collected, analyzed, and disseminated by a number of supporting agencies. A critical issue at this phase is who is in charge. The Army's Special Operations Command (SOCOM) supports the DELTA's training and related operational requirements but, in time of crisis, JSOC bypasses the SOCOM link and directs the unit and the nation's other CT assets. Once deployed, the State Department is the key desision–making element for foreign operations, while the Justice Department deals with problems within the United

National Command Authority

Chairman
Joint Chiefs of Staff

JSOC

SOCOM

DELTA

States. This clean, simple chain of command allows a "stovepipe" of direction and support to the unit and cuts out a number of middlemen who would unintentionally hinder the execution of a mission.

After arriving at the site of the "incident," the next phase deals with preparation. In its simplest form, this means that target surveillance is begun;

outer and inner security rings are checked; command, control and liaison functions are established; and incoming intelligence is analyzed. After all the players are satisfied (or the situation forces the issue), the next phase is the assault, or "takedown," of the objective. Closely on its heels is the swift withdrawal of the force back to their homebase.

With this as background, where does the new trooper fit in? He is likely to fill a number of roles or positions, and his titles may be many. As he progresses within the organization, he will use his past skills and experiences to benefit the team he is assigned to. For example, he may be a sniper because he went to sniper school while assigned to a Ranger battalion. If his demolitions background is good, he may find himself dealing with some very exotic toys designed to blow off the smallest locks or take down the entire wall of a room with minimal disturbance to the occupants of the next room. As a "door kicker" or "shooter," his skills will be fine–tuned in the art of lockpicking, room entry, and target identification. Common phrases often associated with the skills or strengths of these unique professionals include the "double tap," "happiness is a head shot," and "reach out and touch someone."

The SOT provides troopers with various methods of entry, seizure, and exit of terrorist situations. They learn to rappel into second– and third–story windows to get at the terrorists and their victims, as well as how to most effectively kick open a door, use specially manufactured stun grenades to disorient the terrorists and then closely follow the blast into the room. Each member of a four–man team must know not only where he is going, but also precisely where his teammates will be and in which direction their fields of fire are directed.

In this closely orchestrated ballet of death known as close–quarters battle, the troopers learn to pick their targets quickly and then instantly place a minimum of two shots in an eye socket–sized kill zone from as far as fifty feet away. This technique is known as the double tap. Moving quickly through the area, the team learns to secure everyone (regardless of who they are) with plastic flex cuffs and leave the sorting out and medical treatment to the follow–on police forces. These strong, yet pliable, restraining bands not only are easy to use, but a large number can be carried by one man.

It is this type of assault that most people associate with counterterrorist forces. During a takedown, terrorists and hostages alike see only dark apparitions, akin to *Star Wars'* Darth Vader, entering behind the stun or flash/bang grenades. From the top down, every trooper is clad in a modern array of sophisticated armor. Heads are protected by a dark gray or black Kevlar helmet identical to current military issue. Under his "Fritz" helmet is fitted a flame–resistant Nomex balaclava. An earphone and/or microphone provides him instant tactical communication with the rest of the unit. The principle is that everyone involved in the decision–making process and execution must be provided with real–time information in order to control the unfolding operation.

Depending on the situation, a trooper is wearing eye protection in the form of either shatterproof goggles or a protective chemical mask which also provides a degree of eye safety. His upper torso is encased by a Kevlar vest, for gunshot and blast fragmentation protection, over a dark Nomex coverall or a tactical battledress. Over this, a variety of general equipment is worn, along with items that will support his specific tasks. Some troopers will have ammunition and myriad survival aids, such as powerful miniature flashlights and radio receivers. Others will have a variety of grenades, different types of ammo and first–aid equipment or knives. When medical assistance is not likely to be immedi-ately available, CT teams carry a medical pouch containing assorted dressings, IV tubing, saline solutions, and tourniquets.

As with everything else, individual weapons are dictated by the situation. Of course, everyone has a particular favorite, but training on all available CT weapons is a must. Most room entries begin with the lead man using a submachine gun or a semiautomatic pistol. To expedite door–kicking procedures, shotguns firing a sabot or lead slug will be used to blow off the barrier's hinges. Many team members will insist that a submachine gun or shotgun, which can be carried in one hand, is the ideal weapon, and some even mount laser pointers or mini flashlights on their weapons for operations in buildings or dimly lit areas. Plenty of ammo is always strategically placed around his uniform.

Regardless of how much equipment the team member has, each man is aware that one lucky shot or a well–placed booby trap can ruin the best–laid plans. From the soles of his Gore–Tex assault boots to the crown of his Kevlar helmet, a team member's equipment is constantly reviewed and updated. A takedown is an affair that one must come properly dressed for.

Training generally falls into two categories. First the FNG (f——ing new guy) will go through individual skills training designed to break old habits that come from the conventional side of the Army, such as not shooting outside of the prescribed safety limits, and much emphasis is placed on individual action and initiative. New habits, like the double tap, are instilled in the FNG. These come from lessons learned through both successful missions and failures. In the case of the double tap, a pumped–up terrorist in the midst of a takedown cannot be reasoned with or talked into surrendering.

Once this basic training is completed, the FNG enters the team training phase where he is taught how to handle himself in any close–quarters battle,

(**Above**) A CT operative demonstrates how to use a shotgun during a window entry. (**Above right**) A close–up of a "best–case" anchoring system, with abundant safety features. In the heat of a fast–paced takedown, such fine points often have to be bypassed. (**Right and below right**) An assault team conducting a forced entry and room–clearing demonstration of a "hotel conference room." Lock picking is conducted with a charge of C4 plastic explosives. Also note the 360–degree protection and the Walther 9mm P5 pistol and MP-K submachine gun, protective masks, and ballistic (bulletproof) helmets. Expertise with personal weapons while wearing a variety of different equipment combinations is a requirement. (**Below**) If you can't go through the door or a window, go through the wall! Like high tech termites, two US operatives prepare to follow the blast into the next room.

or CQB, whether it is conducted in a building, train, or aircraft. For example, the trooper will be given his first taste of an aircraft takedown at a large mockup of a generic civilian passenger liner at the SOT before training on a great variety of actual aircraft happily supplied by the major carriers at various sites around the country.

Additional CT training is also conducted to teach numerous infiltration methods for moving into isolated target areas. These include parachuting into the area using high–altitude, low–opening (HALO) or high–altitude, high–opening (HAHO), underwater rescue operations using Scuba techniques and miniature submersible vehicles for long–distance travel, and rappelling and fast–roping from helicopters. Teams may also have to learn techniques for driving various types of all–terrain vehicles. Lock-picking is also taught.

Upon completion, the FNG is assigned to a team, and maintenance of his new skills is begun within his troop. Regular cross–training will now occur with related foreign and domestic CT units, such as Britain's SAS or our own Navy SEAL (Sea–Air–Land) teams. Some DELTA troopers will also find themselves temporarily assigned "personal protection duty," providing security to key US personnel, such as ambassadors in Central America and the Middle East.

The Killing House

Take a break you heroes."

The team sergeant chuckles to himself every time he uses that line. If everything is going as it should, his jibe would either cause a rush of sarcastic curses and catcalls or receive a deep–throated moan from the assembled trainees. This time, the muted response indicates that the humid North Carolina weather is having an impact on the strength of the team. More importantly, it was a good indicator of the amount and type of training that should be con-

ducted for the remainder of the day. Based on his observations, the team sergeant decides to deviate from the published training schedule and walk through a room–clearing exercise without the required live ammunition. Training accidents are acceptable in this business but are not sought after.

Fifty meters to the west of this training area, a second and much more experienced team is also working its way through the day's training. Having just finished with their own room–clearing exercise, the men are given one of the most beloved commands in the lexicon of military language: "Take a break."

The break is planned for thirty minutes, but to the team members, it should be longer. Sprawled in various positions underneath the pines, each trooper brushes pine cones out of the way and tries to find a comfortable position while attempting to keep equipment from becoming too dirty with grit and sand. Small rivets of sweat trickle down grimy faces as nomex gloves are removed and calloused hands reach up to brush the sweat away from bloodshot eyes. Each team member wears an assault suit of black Nomex, and some of the team had already removed their black Kevlar helmets and flashproof balaclavas. Goggles, used to provide protection from flying debris, lay in the crown of the helmet, along with sweat–soaked gloves and face masks. Sensitive individual communications earpieces and microphones are inspected to ensure they were switched off.

Each trooper wears body armor, designed to protect throat and chest areas, and "armored shorts" to protect vulnerable groin areas. Some troopers have also added knee and elbow pads under their assault suits, while shin protectors are pulled on by some of the veterans who have grown tired of the bruises and cut shins received in the furniture–cluttered "killing house." Individuals are equipped with either a special–purpose Mossberg automatic shotgun

"Walk–throughs" of room–clearing operations are run with troopers wearing progressively more equipment so the men will gain a clear idea of how different protective sets restrict vision and movement. They must attain extreme levels of proficiency while wearing all combinations of gear. (**Above**) Troopers in coveralls prepare to enter a SOT "killing house" and (**opposite**) perform their ballet of death. Note the mannequin terrorists and hostage in closet.

or a 9mm Heckler & Koch MP5 submachine gun. Most of the free world's CT forces swear by this weapon, and some even argue that it is the best export the Germans have had since *Fräuleins*, Mercedes and beer. In addition to the MP5s, the sniper teams on this exercise are equipped with M24 sniper rifles. Though there are more advanced systems, the accurized Remington 700 bolt–action rifle with five–round fluted, detachable magazine is still the favored standby. Its stainless–steel barrel, and hefty .300 Winchester Magnum round provide this team with the power required to "reach out and touch

someone." All members of the sweeper team carry 9mm Beretta Model 92F pistols: the standard side-arm of the US Army.

While some troopers "smoke and joke," others inhale nourishing liquids from canteens and jugs. Like the fondness each man has for his individual weapons, team members also have a distinct enjoyment of anything liquid. Gatorade, bottled spring water, juices, or just plain H_2O is found in the individual backpacks. Unlike what Hollywood would have one believe, hard–drinking troopers are not the norm. The shakes are not conducive to good teamwork. And to the experienced eye, the soldiers are an organized and tightly knit group of professionals, men who can easily operate as either individuals or a team, making decisions that could have far–reaching impacts at world levels.

"Saddle up, you assholes."

Staff Sergeant Dawkins hated it when the sergeant major tried out his hard, John Wayne voice, and comments sarcastically, "I really wonder if John Wayne ever called anyone an asshole." A number of other uncomplimentary thoughts are voiced as the troopers slowly rise to their feet and adjust their equipment. Gathering around the team leader, Sergeant Major Greg Tusconey, the men fall in to form a loose formation facing their boss.

Looking up from his notebook, Sergeant Major Tusconey begins with an in–depth critique of the morning's past exercise. He cites their strengths as well as their weaknesses. When finished, he faces his soldiers and says in a matter–of–fact tone, "OK, girls, let's get our shit together and try it again." The resounding reply to the implication that there is a collective lack of masculinity within the unit is indicative of a team who can give as much as it can take.

Sauntering back to their briefing area, the team members arrange themselves on wooden benches placed in front of a graphic representation of the

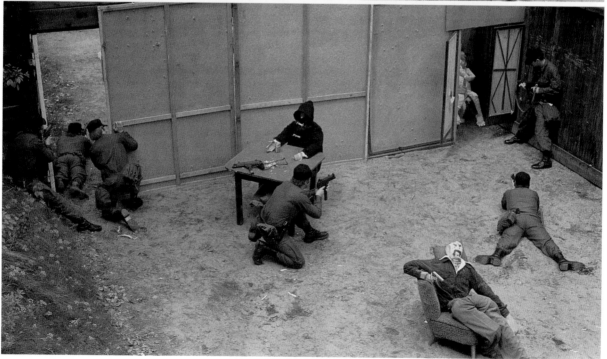

rooms within the killing house. A key factor in these exercises, as well as an actual assault, is the need for critical, accurate, and up–to–date information about the physical layout of the passenger aircraft or building, as well as the locations of the hostages and their terrorist keepers. Stepping up in front of the diagram, the sergeant major begins to describe the mission for the team in clear, concise, and pointed terms:

"At 1730 hours last night, terrorists assaulted the US Embassy, and took sixteen State Department employees as hostages. Two US Marines were killed during the initial assault. We are to prepare for a deliberate takedown of the building on order from higher." Stopping to scan the team for questions, he continues. "Outer security has been established by the local police, and inner security has been established by the hasty response team from the 10th Special Forces Group until after we arrive and take over responsibility for the mission. Recon of the building has been conducted, along with a debrief of our people and the locals who have solid, current intel."

Tusconey proceeds to outline the rehearsal schedules and timetables, who is responsible for what, and how he envisions the takedown will be accomplished. After the thorough briefing is completed, individual troopers are quizzed and then individual and team rehearsals are begun. As the last rays of the fading sun are engulfed by the approach of a cool, wet front, the last preparations are wound up. For this exercise, the chopper support for the takedown will come from "the Task Force" as the 160th SOAR is usually referred to.

The team is divided into sniper and assault elements, which coordinate the operation's precise timing, and move out. The two sniper teams each consist of a spotter and a shooter. They are linked together with the assault team, sweeper team, and command center by radio. Each sniper team moves along individual routes previously reconned and takes positions offering vantage points overlooking the target area. The assault element, meanwhile, is moving toward their pickup zone, or PZ, to rendezvous with an inbound chopper. The word circulates that the order has been received. The mission is on.

Because the operation will take place at night, infrared reflective tape is added to each member's equipment. Strips are applied around the chest, wrists, ankles and helmet. Using AN/PVS-7 night vision goggles (NVGs), all assault members will be easily seen in the heat of night combat. The sun has long ago set, and a steady drizzle falls through the tall pines as the team divides evenly and prepares to board the chopper. Right on schedule, the air is disturbed by the pounding of rotor blades beating the heavy night mist. Like a giant dragonfly, the MH-60 Black Hawk glides into the PZ, where the team immediately loads through the side doors. The pilot's eyes are unaided but his copilot wears aviator's AN/AVS-6 NVGs. Immediately, the team leader places the spare set of headphones over his ears and communicates with the pilot.

"Evening," says the pilot in a slow, Southern drawl.

"How's it going?" replies the sergeant major.

Formalities exhausted, Tusconey quickly briefs the aircrew on how the team will carry out the infil as the aircraft nears the target. Due to the lousy weather, the landing zone, or LZ, will be the building's sloping rooftop, and the team will drop onto a very small area at its peak, where a flat space had been located during photo recon analysis. Normally, the team would rappel or fast–rope in, but the wet weather and reduced visibility give them an added advantage and they'll be able to get closer to the target. With clockwork precision, the Black Hawk angles into the rooftop LZ and flares out level and steady. Looking through his NVGs, Tusconey sees that everyone is ready and in a low, distinct voice says, "Stand by, stand by." Prompted by his warning, the sniper teams report in: "Sniper One, ready. Target sighted." "Sniper Two ready. No target." At his hand signal, the lead team members prepare to exit. Taking a deep breath, he gives the command, "Go!"

The soldiers leap onto the mist–shrouded roof and fan out across its tricky incline in a predetermined (and well–rehearsed) pattern. Almost as quickly as the bird arrived at the LZ, it disappears into the gloom. Two team members attach green nylon climbing ropes to anchor points, drop them over the sides of the building along predetermined entry sites, and kneel in anticipation after attaching their snaplinks. Six other men move to a rooftop door and, after determining that it is locked, move into a tight file along the outside wall. The door hinges will have to be shot off.

The Number One man, armed with a Mossberg 12–gauge shotgun, prepares to blast the offending hinges off the wooden door. Despite the fact that every soldier is in communication with the rest of the team, discipline is absolute and the only sound breaking the silence is the constant hiss over each man's earpiece.

It has been ten seconds since the team landed. At the command, "Go!" the hinges disintegrate in a shower of sparks and splinters as the shotgun's solid lead slug crashes into each hinge, starting with the top and working down. Yanking the door to the side, the Number Two trooper rapidly steps into the doorway, where he immediately places his back to the dimly lit stairwell wall. Sweeping the staircase with his NVG, he breathlessly alerts follow–on troopers to the situation he is observing. Number Three now bursts through the doorway and in calculated steps moves down the stairs and secures the top floor stairwell. Peering down the hallway, he speaks in clear, crisp, and rapid tones into his micro-

phone: "Number Three, hallway clear." Trooper Number Four is immediately at his side, having followed his partner down the stairs. As Number Three moves to the right, Number Four moves left and blends into the darkened hallway. Both troopers' H&Ks move in measured arcs: ceiling to floor, left to right. Whenever a trooper's eyes move under their NVG, the stubby barrel of his MP5 follows, ready to spit out a lethal three–round burst along that same visual arc.

The second assault element of four men moves along the right side of the hallway toward a door on the right. The lead man (Number Three) senses motion in the room. Reaching down along his left thigh, he extracts a pop can–sized flash/bang grenade from his leg pouch. Bringing it up to his right hand, which still clutches an MP5, he slides the grenade's pullring over his right hand's gloved thumb. While holding the safety spoon, he pulls the ring. Gently rolling the grenade into the room, he flattens himself against the wall as he warns his teammates. "Grenade" reverberates through the soldier's earphones and, almost immediately, "Go!" is commanded before the nonlethal grenade has expended its package.

Number Five slides into the left side of the doorway as the room erupts in multiple flashes and explosions designed to disrupt, disorientate and illuminate. As he moves through the door, Number Six follows and slides into the black, smoke–filled room along the doorway's right wall. He is followed by Numbers Seven and Eight who had entered the floor through windows on the other side of the building. Number Seven backs Number Five by taking on any targets from his twelve– through three–o'clock (the right hand wall). Number Five already has acquired a target through his NVG in his twelve– through nine–o'clock area along the left wall.

A masked terrorist is wildly trying to bring his Polish–made AK-47 assault rifle to bear on a young

(**Above**) A team wearing ballistic helmets takes up position along the wall, to avoid being silhouetted against an open door, as their shooter takes aim at a European–style door latch with a pump shotgun. (**Opposite**) After entry, the team fans out along the walls before picking targets.

woman strapped to a chair near the center of the office. Number Five squeezes a three–round burst into the throat of the terrorist, who goes down in a spasmatic heap.

As Number Seven checks the terrorist for other weapons and vital signs, Number 5 maintains a steady aim on the lifeless corpse. Flipping the terrorist over on his stomach, Number Seven expertly

pins his wrists together with flex cuffs. After a quick check of the room, Numbers Six and Eight now check the bound female for booby traps. More than one rescue has ended in disaster when the rescuers failed to check for explosives secreted somewhere on a hostage. A grenade or stick of dynamite can turn a rescue into a sticky affair. After the check is completed, the team exits the room. Eight seconds have passed. As the leader leaves, he announces "Number Two, one terrorist down, one hostage secured, main room, top floor" to the command post and the other team members. Now it is up to the sweepers and backup police forces to take charge of the room.

This ballet of death will continue until the "embassy" is cleared of terrorists and all the hostages are accounted for. After the team exits the building, they move to an assembly area and are whisked away for an in–depth debriefing. If this had been a real takedown, actual terrorists and hostages would be considerably more unpredictable than the mannequins and pop–up targets the team had to deal with. Local police and medical personnel, as well as the sweepers, would have also been moving simultaneously through the building to deal with the carnage left behind and make a complete record of what happened. It may have to be used later as evidence.

This is a typical exercise.

During such exercises, the trooper is trained not to fall into the Rambo approach to CT operations: Never fire from the hip and always extend your folding stock. Fire at close range and don't waste ammo. You learn how to move: dropping to a crouch, firing, dropping and firing again, and moving to the next position. You learn to move quickly through doorways and get in position and maintain proper trigger control.

Chapter 4
Decade of Frustration

General [Bernard] Rogers told me of a note from the President. It had surfaced in the tank earlier in the day [October 18,1977] and asked, "Do we have the same capability as the West Germans?" Much discussion ensued before it was decided that we did not. One of the generals present had said, "Well I'm not going over to the White House and tell him we don't."

Colonel Charlie A. Beckwith, US Army (Retired)

Throughout the 1980s, DELTA was beset by a number of events that might have caused lesser organizations to collapse. The troopers trained hard but were seldom deployed. They watched helplessly as Americans were whisked from streets and university offices in Beirut and seized in large groups in hijacked airliners and ships. Worse yet, the men found themselves gearing up for rescue operations that were cancelled time and again for a variety of reasons. During this same period, the unit also found themselves on the receiving end of a disturbing amount of unwanted publicity. In addition to a highly publicized financial scandal involving DELTA members, the easy visual access to the Special Operations Training Facility (SOT) may have been a factor in the media's knowledge of deployments during several hostage crises.

A US flag burns on the Rhein–Main Air Base perimeter fence during a period of mass left–wing demonstrations and terrorist strikes against American targets in Germany.

Although it's shocking to think that a unit on the cutting edge of America's war on terrorism was—and still is—in appearance at least, so vulnerable, it was only the tip of the weak links plaguing counterterrorism. In addition to the expected security problems associated with CT operations, numerous interdepartmental squabbles and convoluted command and control issues abounded. An excellent example concerned justification for CT operations within the continental United States. The Justice Department's Federal Bureau of Investigation is responsible for tackling terrorist incidents at home, yet DELTA had to provide badly needed assistance during both the 1986 Statue of Liberty centennial in New York City and the 1984 Olympics in Los Angeles in spite of numerous jurisdictional and legal problems.

When CT operations are planned for overseas, numerous diplomatic issues become critical elements in the military/political equation, and the State Department steps to the forefront. Probably

(**Above**) US and GSG-9 counterterrorists conducting joint training at a West German site. A classic procedure in building clearing is for a team to rappel to a roof from a helicopter, then work its way from top to bottom, outside to inside. Such operations require split–second timing and in–depth coordination. Note that this special ops UH-1N Huey, though painted black for night operations, is clearly marked as an American military helicopter for any German operatives taking part in a joint takedown. (**Right**) After rappeling down the building side, a US operative prepares to enter a window. His teammate has already successfully completed this tricky maneuver. During actual operations, there is always the risk that an unexpected greeting awaits the team. (**Opposite page**) "Steady as she goes." A US trooper gives a German counterterrorist a hand before he disappears over the edge.

the most basic question that must be asked before contemplating operations on foreign turf is: What sovereign nation wants to relinquish command and control to United States military forces conducting such highly visible operations on their soil? It has to be remembered that no matter how discreetly DELTA may conduct itself in the run–up to an operation, every hostage rescue is undeniably a high–visibility operation *after* its well–publicized conclusion. The implication for the nation hosting DELTA is, of course, that it does not have the re-

sources to take care of its own internal problems. The domestic, as well as international, political ramifications for a government can be enormous. Add to this mess the fact that the Joint Special Operations Command, the direct link between DELTA and the president (known as the National Command Authority) and the Joint Chiefs of Staff (JCS), can receive marching orders from both. The JCS is better qualified to oversee any operations involving DELTA, but common sense remained a missing ingredient in this war, as can be seen by the less–than–desirable results in Grenada.

Aftermath

The fallout from the inferno of *Desert I* was complicated and far reaching. Not only did President Jimmy Carter lose his bid for re–election, but Egypt's supportive president, Anwar Sadat (who was already on a number of hit lists for his part in the Camp David Accords), was now a principal target of Iranian–sponsored fanatics for allowing the "Great Satan" to launch Operation *Eagle Claw* from his country. He would soon die at the hands of Muslim fundamentalists.

JCS planners continued their work, and soon a new mission to rescue the hostages in Iran, code–named *Honey Badger,* was put together under the direction of the renowned and much–respected General Richard Secord. Armed with the proper special operations support—and the hard–learned lessons gleaned from *Eagle Claw*— he assembled a powerful force of special operations aviators, Special Forces and DELTA troopers, intelligence collectors, and agents who were prepared to go it again. But it was not meant to be. Some two minutes after Ronald Reagan was sworn in as President of the United States, the hostages were released.

To help dampen the firestorm of criticism that erupted after *Desert I*, a six–officer review group was appointed by the chairman of the JCS, General David C. Jones. It was chaired by Admiral James L. Holloway, and the balance of its membership consisted of generals from the Army, Air Force, and Marines who had experience in either special or clandestine operations.

These investigators came to the conclusion that *Eagle Claw* was plagued by untested operational methods, poor communications procedures, and a dangerously informal command structure lacking unity of command. Training for the mission, moreover, had been conducted by its various compo-

nents at different sites without a full dress rehearsal using all the assigned elements—something that would have highlighted the most glaring operational and equipment shortfalls. The commission recommended that "a permanent field agency" of the JCS be established with "assigned staff personnel and certain assigned forces" and that a "murder board" of military experts be formed to independently examine mission plans before execution.

As for Colonel Beckwith, he was asked by General Meyer to formalize an earlier proposal for a permanently operating joint task force that would fall directly under the JCS and combine dedicated Army, Navy, and Air Force elements during its training and planning. Beckwith and others had long voiced the opinion that this type of organization was needed, and Major General John Singlaub put it best when he stated *Eagle Claw* didn't work because "we tried to bring disparate units from all over the Armed Forces—from all over the world—and then put them into an ad hoc arrangement to

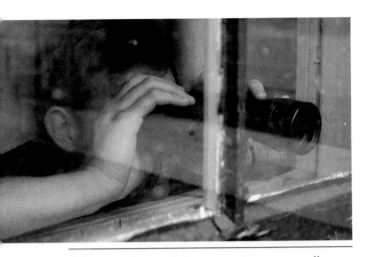

A key ingredient in CT operations is covert intelligence collection. Here, an intel specialist supports a DELTA training mission by conducting surveillance operations from a concealed site.

do a very complicated plan."

Beckwith's proposal to establish a Joint Special Operations Command (JSOC) was approved by Meyer in May 1980, and he was soon transferred from DELTA to the newly formed, independent organization he helped create. He badly missed the excitement of leading a combat team, though, and remarked that his staff billet "ain't as good a job [as DELTA]." He retired to the Lone Star State in 1981 and opened a security service. Harkening back to his days with Britain's Special Air Service, he gave his company the name SAS of Texas.

The establishment of the JSOC was one of many honest attempts to put teeth in America's counterterrorist effort in the wake of *Desert I*. As expected, the new government programs became battlegrounds for interdepartmental squabbles. The major catalyst for this fighting was, of course, money since counterterrorism was now in vogue and took funding away from other programs.

DELTA's friends in high places went to even higher places, and the post–Beckwith organization thrived during this period. The unit's strength before *Eagle Claw* of just over 100 men, making up two small A and B squadrons plus support, grew to a relatively stable force of 300 during the early 1980s— enough for three full–sized squadrons— with its selection and training as brutally efficient as ever. The unit also benefited greatly from production of *Task, Conditions and Standards for DELTA*, or, as it is more commonly known, "the Black Book." This document was produced only because General Meyer essentially grabbed Beckwith by the shoulders, pushed him down into a chair, and forced him to compose it.

Meyer, now the Army's chief of staff, was anxious that DELTA not reinvent the wheel with each new commander and wanted to ensure that it would retain its SAS–type structure, one that is unique within the US Army. Four troops of approximately sixteen men make up a squadron, with each troop able to reconfigure itself into eight–, six–, four–, three–, or two–soldier teams or elements. This degree of flexibility is one of the key ingredients in DELTA's ability to handle virtually any terrorist scenario.

DELTA also moved its headquarters from the old post stockade to the new, state–of–the–art SOT, appropriately nicknamed "Wally World" after a lavish theme park in the *National Lampoon's Vacation* movie. But, in a sense, it wasn't just DELTA that came up a big winner from the increased awareness of the terrorist threat. The whole military benefitted because it was identified as the obvious candidate to receive the now readily available funds. And the funds did flow: to Air Force special operations, Navy SEALs, Army aviation, Rangers, and Special Forces, as well as a large supporting cast in the various services, such as the Army's Intelligence Support Activity (ISA).

The State Department, however, was soon to emerge as the biggest winner. Being in the best position to judge the political ramifications of US actions on a host nation's territory, it received the responsibility for overseeing all overseas counter-terrorist operations. But despite the fact that the United States now had its CT apparatus well-organized and in place, the future proved to be not so rosy as the optimists hoped.

Operation *Urgent Fury*

After Ronald Reagan assumed the presidency in 1981, he "let it be known to friend and foe alike" that he had learned from the hard lessons of his predecessors. Surrounded by capable and, in some cases, hawkish advisors, President Reagan was determined that, like the sheriffs of the Old West, he would clean up the world and make it safe for women and children. All he needed was a place to start and the force to sweep up the mess. He didn't have long to wait. At the southern end of the Antilles chain lies the beautiful Caribbean island of Grenada. A former ward of the British Empire, this idyllic eight- by fifteen-mile island was to be the testing ground for the new president and the changes that had been made in the special operations community since *Desert I*.

On October 19, 1983, Grenada's Marxist prime minister, Maurice Bishop, and several cabinet members were lined up along the walls of old Fort Rupert and executed by former associates who formed an even more radical "Revolutionary Military Counsel." Bishop had aligned himself with the Soviets and their Cuban surrogates, who had, among other things, constructed a large military communications facility, a 10,000-foot runway capable of handling long-range transports, and extensive airfield support facilities, ostensibly to support its meager tourist industry. While a single air base would not allow a hostile force to control the entrance into the southern Caribbean during a war, it would provide an excellent stopover for aircraft bringing in material and personnel support for "peoples' revolutions" in Central and South America.

MH-6 Little Birds of the 160th SOAR operating in the Persian Gulf. Among other operations they took part in was the September 1987 capture of an Iranian mine-laying vessel that threatened oil tanker traffic.

With the execution of the genuinely popular leader, widespread protests broke out on the island, and when the military opened fire on the demonstrators, the die was cast. The threat to the region caused an uproar among the neighboring Caribbean nations, and the Reagan administration believed that a radical, Marxist government (that thought nothing of shooting its own citizens) would, sooner or later, get around to using the roughly 600 American students at the island's medical school as pawns in a dangerous game to keep the US military from closing down the airfield. The young students were a hostage situation waiting to happen, so the United States moved quickly to launch Operation *Urgent Fury*.

Leading the assaults were several of the US military's elite as well as (until then) classified units. UH-60 Black Hawks of Task Force (TF) 160 flew directly from the United States to a nearby island launch site, with the help of additional internal fuel tanks, while MH-6s were brought in by Air Force cargo planes. During the early morning hours of

65

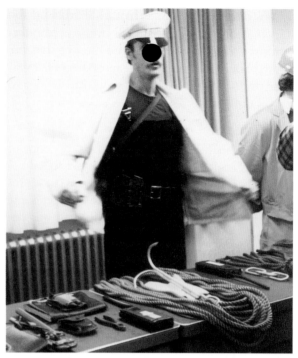

Counterterrorist specialists must be able to use any ruse or disguise to get close to hostage holding sites, such as an aircraft or buildings. Here, US Army CT operatives display equipment and various disguises during a briefing for General Bernard Rogers, Supreme Allied Commander, Europe, in the early 1980s. (**Left**) One of the typical "European businessmen" holsters his 9mm Beretta pistol and (**right**) a "street cleaner," standing beside a "municipal worker," shows off his protective vest and ammunition belt. Note the equipment on display.

October 25, the expert aviators of TF 160 ferried their ground counterparts, DELTA, to targets near the airfield at Point Salines, where they were to carry out a direct action mission ahead of two Ranger battalions parachuting in at dawn. Their target was the airfield control facilities which, it turned out, were heavily ringed by misplaced, but marginally effective, automatic weapons. A second mission entailed the takedown of Richmond Hill Prison, where one Black Hawk was lost to Soviet–made

ZSU-23-2 (twin 23mm) antiaircraft guns. In both cases, men and aircraft were lost (some figures are still classified). The lack of timely, on–the–spot, intelligence had again raised its ugly head.

Several members of the elite Navy SEAL Team 6 have privately related that they had an especially rough time as DELTA and the TF 160 units were running into their own problems in the south. One deadly incident occurred when four of their members parachuted into rough seas to conduct a linkup with a surface vessel that was to take them in close for a water infiltration. The drowning of these four men did not stop the mission, but it did tragically demonstrate that even the best of the best are sometimes incapable of overcoming the odds.

A major concern during *Urgent Fury* was the safety of the British government's representative. Tasked to keep the gentleman from falling into the hands of the Grenadan "Peoples' Revolutionary

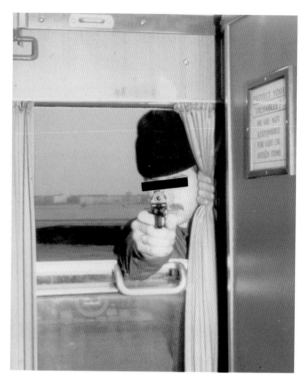

(**Above**) Unlike situations depicted in movies, actual aircraft takedowns must be accomplished quickly, violently, and with surgical precision. Here, a suspected hijacker in a mock airliner cabin is controlled the best way: with a pistol to the head. (**Right**) "Tickets please!" A terrorist's view of a US operative taken during a train–clearing exercise in Europe.

Armed Forces," twenty–two other members of SEAL Team 6 flew in by chopper, fast–roped onto the rooftop and grounds of the governor's residence, and took control. A stunned Grenadan defense unit located nearby summoned help from two Soviet supplied BTR-60 armored personnel carriers mounting multiple machine guns. The sudden appearance of substantial hostile elements forced the planned evacuation of Government House to be hastily cancelled. They were, as one SEAL member later described, "in a world 'a shit" and had to fight in place. With neither antiarmor weapons nor good communications, the team held out as best they could until a Specter gunship came to their rescue and eliminated the problem. But even with the help of the AC-130's massive firepower, up to half of the rescue party is reported to have been wounded by the time Marines reached them on the second day of *Urgent Fury.*

Months later, a veteran SEAL discussing the operation sighed after draining his beer and said, "Thank God it was just the Grenadans." When pressed, he continued, "Every time some nonqualified son of a bitch plans or directs our operations, we get our asses handed to us on a silver platter. It just ain't right." Right or wrong, the end result from the problems of *Urgent Fury* was that closer control over the planning of special operations would, at least for a while, be handled by people who "had been there," which means thoroughly qualified in special operations planning.

An interesting wrinkle on special operations on Grenada came from the media's coverage of *Urgent Fury.* Although the Army had refused to either confirm or deny the use of special operations forces for nearly eight years, ABC News was able to extract a concession that one TF 160 captain was killed and eleven DELTA troopers injured after broadcasting footage of the downing of his Black Hawk— an event previously unaccounted for in the Pentagon recap of the operation. An American resident of Grenada had shot the film; other footage showed MH-6s, aircraft for which no procurement information had been publicly released. They were identified by ABC News as Hughes 500 helicopters, its civilian designation.

After the operation, increasingly bitter complaints over the "veil of secrecy" surrounding special operations were heard from some quarters of the media. Also being made was the highly dubious claim that only the American public was being denied access to information since the Soviets supposedly already knew all about such activities. While this is a subject that will certainly never be concluded to everyone's satisfaction, it is an undeniable fact that even relatively low losses can have a severe impact on the capabilities of a small unit. And if the small unit performs a mission of vital strategic importance, that loss may be magnified a hundred-fold. Not only do Western intelligence agencies monitor terrorist networks, but the terrorists themselves monitor CT organizations, with the assistance of various friendly governments that track Western units and capabilities largely through press reports and, occasionally, espionage. It is not in the best interests of the United States to reveal losses in key covert units within days—or even months—after they were suffered. In this case, freedom of information must take a back seat to security

Trouble in the Mediterranean

Almost immediately on the heels of *Urgent Fury*, members of Italy's own homespun terrorist organization, the Red Brigade, abducted an American one-star general named James L. Dozier from his apartment on December 17, 1982. Authorities were later to learn that Dozier was not the intended victim, but, instead, a Navy admiral had been the group's actual target. Regardless of who was snatched, the impact all over Europe was the same: NATO military facilities soon became prison camps for the Allies. Virtually every senior officer seemed to see himself or his family as a prime target for the terrorists.

Against this background of confusion, the experts from various special operations units converged on Italy. Much to their credit, the Italians told everyone to kindly go home since this was their turf. But while all door kickers were sent packing, they did keep some special operators who could assist with such exotic needs as radio and telephone intercept.

When the alarm was sounded, one of the units offered was the European Command's own hasty response detachment. Its commander found himself on the first plane into the area. He was also on the first plane out. The Italians recognized incompetence when they saw it, and had enough problems of their own without having to wet–nurse a rookie counterterrorist in addition to the US State Department. With the help of the US signal intercept folks, the Italians found and rescued the kidnapped general, and American CT "experts" learned one

General Dozier's kidnappers erected a tent inside a safe-house room to hold their prisoner. (**Opposite**) Dozier displays a diagram of the tent and nearest guard position after Italian counterterrorists forcibly freed him from the Red Brigade. (**Above**) Lebanese rescue workers and US Marines gather outside the flattened Marine barracks in the aftermath of a terrorist truck bombing. The suicide driver had driven directly past Marine guards, who had been ordered not to carry loaded weapons. There were lessons to be learned: Listen to the warnings of counterterrorist specialists, plus shoot first and worry about CNN later.

more lesson in dealing with the real world.

In 1982, Iran had sent roughly 2,000 of their fanatical Revolutionary Guards to the Lebanese free–for–all civil war as "volunteers." While a good number of them would go to paradise after falling in regular combat against Christian militiamen (and leftist Shiites and Druz militiamen and renegade Palestinians and US Marine snipers, as well as Israeli, Lebanese, and Syrian soldiers), a select few were destined to meet Allah in a less conventional man-

The television image of a TWA pilot being prevented from talking with reporters by an armed hijacker at Beirut airport in June 1985.

ner. These "martyrs" drove explosives–laden trucks into barracks, embassies, or other high–priority targets. On the night of April 18, 1983, forty French paratroopers and 241 US Marines were killed by a pair of these truck bombers after failing to heed the lessons of a similar attack earlier that year on a US Embassy building.

Another incident in late October of that year concerned members of the 10th Special Forces Group who were billeted in a downtown hotel while training and advising the Lebanese Army. The group's commander, Colonel Richard Potter, was warned by associates with connections to the Shiite fundamentalists that the group's quarters were targeted for yet another suicide bombing. Potter, DELTA's former deputy commander and a veteran of *Desert I*, was not about to let such warnings go unheeded and immediately moved his force to a Lebanese Army base north of the city. In this case, the training of one man, along with past friendships nurtured over years of frustration, spared the wives of the 10th Special Forces a visit from a chaplain and the ever present survivor assistance officer.

On December 4, 1984, DELTA was sent to assault a Kuwaiti airliner hijacked on its way to Pakistan. Two American passengers were killed during the incident, and the aircraft was forced to fly to Iran, where both the terrorists and hostages were released before the unit could intervene. Six months later, on June 14, the unit was sent back to the region in preparation for an assault on TWA Flight 847, but the affair ended before they could be employed; one off-duty Navy serviceman on board was singled out and murdered. DELTA failed to come to grips

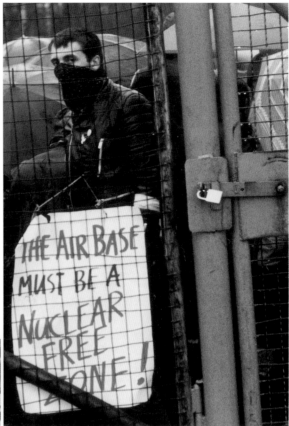

Throughout the 1970s and 1980s, terrorists in Germany were like fish swimming in a great sea of militant leftist/ Marxist/ecologist/misfit/nationalist extremists and sympathizers. (**Right**) A masked demonstrator protesting outside the US air base at Rhein–Main and (**below**), an arms cache believed to have been hidden by Germany's Red Army Faction. Terrorist groups rely heavily on hidden caches of arms and other supplies.

with terrorists again in October, during the *Achille Lauro* affair, and the resulting fiasco at Sigonella Naval Air Station, Sicily, pointed out that the Italians were not about to change their position on whether they or the Americans have jurisdiction on Italian turf. Members of SEAL Team 6 attempted to take the hijackers into custody and were re-

minded that they were not the ones in charge.

The Palestinian extremists who commandeered the Italian vessel had been persuaded to leave it at Alexandria, Egypt, in return for safe conduct to friendly Tunisia, where the PLO maintained its headquarters. They boarded a commercial passenger jet and left Egypt immediately ahead of DELTA's arrival but was quickly intercepted by US F-14 Tomcat fighters, which diverted it to the US–Italian air base. Once the airliner was forced to land, it was quickly surrounded by the SEALs, who were, in turn, surrounded by Italian *carabonari*, who also blocked their C-141 with security vehicles. Since both groups were attempting to carry out their orders and

71

(**Above**) The unmarked limousine of General Frederick Krossen, commander of US Army forces in Europe, after a failed assassination attempt by Germany's Red Army Faction in September 1981. Only a month before, the general had finally heeded the advice of West German counterterrorists and obtained the special armored Mercedes that deflected the blast of the Soviet–made rocket–propelled grenade away from the car's interior. In the car was the general, his wife, an aid, and a German driver/bodyguard. (**Right**) A West German wanted poster for known terrorists. As various fugitives were apprehended or killed, they were crossed off the poster by the US CT team that mounted it on their headquarters' wall.

apprehend the hijackers, a tense situation developed between the senior US officer present and Italian officers. The situation quickly degenerated and the *carabonari* loaded and locked their trusty Berettas and drew down on the equally well–armed SEALs. It was an Italian standoff until the diplomats intervened and determined that it was in ev-

eryone's best interest to let the Italians take charge.

Yet another incident occurred the following month, when a commercial airliner was hijacked to Malta by Palestinian extremists. This time, DELTA was on hand but not used. In fact, they were initially not even allowed to land. Since the hijacked aircraft was Egyptian, that country's commandos, trained by US special operations personnel, were allowed to conduct the takedown. It turned sour, and fifty–seven hostages lost their lives.

Troubles at Home

From 1970 through the mid–1980s, more than 1,000 Americans had been killed, taken hostage, or otherwise injured by foreign terrorists. Virtually all of these incidents had occurred overseas, but CT planners believed that America's luck might not hold out much longer: The upcoming 1984 Summer Olympics to be held in Los Angeles was an awfully tempting target. As part of the $1 billion effort to provide security from possible attacks, DELTA deployed to a nearby naval facility and stood ready to counter any terrorist situation. Along with DELTA was a massive CT force incorporating city and state SWAT (special weapons and tactics) teams and the Federal Bureau of Investigation's Hasty Response Team, commonly referred to as HURT. All were given varying degrees of responsiblity to counter threats, depending on their level of expertise and available manpower.

One interesting sidenote to DELTA's deployment at the Olympics was their use of a mobile command post disguised as a Budweiser beer truck for surreptitiously transporting a response team to the site of an incident. While mention of such a vehicle almost invariably brings snickers to the mouths of listeners accustomed to seeing similar tricks on scores of television cop shows and films as diverse as *Good Neighbor Sam* and *Stripes*, the fact remains that a vehicle camouflaged in this unconventional manner looks like it "belongs" and can move virtually unnoticed if that is what is required. Thankfully, the truck was not needed, but it had to be a comforting sight to those in the know.

Unlike the funds spent on producing the Budweiser truck, not all monies funneled through Army covert accounts were spent wisely or even legitimately. Army auditors discovered a number of irregularities in a covert account between 1981 and 1983. A disturbing amount of double–dipping had taken place and such items as a hot–air balloon and Rolls–Royce sedan had been purchased supposedly to support clandestine operations.

In a climate that one DELTA member described as "sheer hysteria," standard cost–accounting techniques were applied to ongoing covert operations and training. The result was dozens of reprimands and perhaps a score or more transfers resulting from nonjudicial punishments in lieu of court–martials. Some soldiers, however, were not so lucky. Nor did they deserve to be. In one case, an ISA lieutenant colonel, who supported DELTA set up a firm named Business Security International as a conduit for covert funds and misappropriated more than $50,000 in just six months. In a series of discreet courts martial and a civil criminal trial running through 1986, at least two officers were "assigned to the long course" and are still serving prison terms at Leavenworth Penitentiary.

For most DELTA troopers, though, life remained at its grueling, hurry–up–and–wait pace. Troopers continued their meticulous training and provided advice and support to CT units around the world as they did during the Los Angeles Olympics, when a team was quickly dispatched to Willemstad, Curacao, in the Dutch Antilles, to assist in the takedown of a hijacked Venezuelan DC-9. Both fanatics were killed and seventy–nine passengers were freed. Meanwhile, in Lebanon, kidnappings continued unabated and two of the hostages were murdered, CIA station chief William Buckley in 1985 and Marine Colonel William Higgins in 1989. Frequent changes in hostage holding sites and lack of solid US intelligence sources within the terrorists' camp prevented rescues from being undertaken, and at least one major operation involving DELTA and the SEALs was scrubbed. The professionals at DELTA were, in effect, all dressed up with no place to go. Sometimes, though, this was distinctly good news— as was the case when New York City's vulnerable Statue of Liberty centennial celebration passed without a hitch in July 1986.

On other occasions, events took care of themselves— as in San Salvador and Manila. On November 21, 1989, DELTA was dispatched to the Salvadoran capital of San Salvador to rescue Green

West Berlin police sifting through the rubble of the La Belle discotheque, a bar popular with American servicemen, where a soldier and Turkish woman were killed by a bomb. Intelligence analysts soon discovered that the explosives were planted by Libyan agents based out of their embassy in communist East Berlin.

Beret trainers trapped in the Sheraton Hotel during a guerrilla offensive. The trainers escaped unharmed, however, before the detachment could be put into action. Almost two weeks later, DELTA received another alert for a possible rescue attempt, this time in the Philippines. American citizens were again trapped, this time by an Army coup d'état, but emerged unscathed when the revolt fizzled.

Berlin presented a more interesting—and longlasting—problem for US, as well as British and French, CT units stationed in the city's Western sectors. Along the seven crossing points through the Wall between East and West, Communist East German border guards, called *Vopos*, checked passports to prevent East Germans from passing into the West, while the British, French, and American guards allowed people to pass unimpeded both ways since they didn't, for political reasons, view East Berlin as a "foreign" territory. A situation was thus created where potential terrorists, finding some access restrictions from Western nations, could simply cross into the city from East Berlin, where the Syrians, Lybians, Iranians, and even the PLO, maintained diplomatic missions. A US hasty response team was always on a high state of alert and an active exchange program was conducted with DELTA. They operated in close conjunction with Berlin's other Western security organizations, but could not prevent terrorist attacks like the April 5, 1986, bombing of the La Belle discotheque, a club frequented by many American servicemen, in which two people were killed and 230 others were injured. The twilight world of terrorism and counterterrorism, espionage and counterespionage, did not end until the East German communist system finally collapsed of its own weight, bringing the Berlin Wall down with it.

Throughout it all, the frustrations and false starts, DELTA troopers maintained their high degree of professionalism and managed to keep their sometimes–irreverent sense of humor. All knew that the beeper clipped to their belts could sound its annoying electronic bleep at any time to signal a recall and they'd casually drop whatever they were doing with an offhand, "Looks like it's time to head on back to the Ranch,"* and disappear out the door for who knows how long.

*The affection of some shaggy–haired troopers for Levis, chewing tobacco, and cowboy boots led their original headquarters at Fort Bragg's old stockade to be called "the Ranch," and even after the unit moved to its new digs at Wally World, the name persisted.

(**Top**) The US Army's hasty response team in Berlin and several DELTA troopers pose for a group photo during a break in a training exercise. (**Above**) During antiterrorist training in West Berlin, an American serviceman is "snatched" by a group of mock terrorists.

Operation *Just Cause*

A public affairs release from Operation *Just Cause* stated simply that all units from the "special operations command participated" in the operation. DELTA's most publicized mission was the rescue of an American businessman and Rotary Club member held in Panama's notorious Modelo Prison. Kurt Muse was a resident of Panama and, in concert with fellow Panamanian Rotarians (dubbed the "Rotarians from Hell" by *Soldier of Fortune* magazine), had been causing Panama's strongman, Manuel Noriega, trouble by operating a clandestine radio station, filling the air waves with propaganda and, in some instances, reporting misleading or confusing instructions to the Panamanian Defense Forces (PDF) on military radio frequencies. Muse was eventually turned in by the wife of a former co-conspirator and was jailed at Modelo, located a stone's throw from Noriega's command post/headquarters turned fortress called the *Comandancia*.

In the early morning hours of December 19, 1989, Muse was rescued by members of DELTA in a classic CT operation. Transported to the rooftop of the prison by an MH-6, the assault team, backed up by a man on the inside who disabled the facility's emergency generator, cleared the upper floors from the top down and fought their way to the cell holding area where Muse was imprisoned. White beams of light from the troopers' weapon–mounted pointers pierced the smoke–filled cell, after its door was blown, and Muse was whisked to the roof up a darkened stairwell as Specter gunships pummeled the *Comandancia* across the street.

Armed with MP5s of various configurations, the troopers took out the armed guards with lethal shock and firepower and used just enough explosives to open the door without harming Muse. The waiting MH-6 was piloted by a lone soldier from the 160th SOAR. Two troopers fought their way to Muse's cell, two more provided security on the stairwell, and four more were on the roof, exchanging fire with prison guards in the barracks beyond a small courtyard. The operation, so far, had unfolded with the clockwork precision of a Wally World exercise. As the security and rescue teams loaded into the helo and along its outside–mounted seats, the heavily laden Little Bird lifted into the night sky.

What Muse saw was as close to a living hell as Wagnerian opera. AC-130s were tearing great chunks out of the *Comandancia's* defenses, while tracers streamed upward at buzzing Black Hawk helicopters and, in the streets below, conventional mechanized infantry forces brought maximum pressure to bear on the PDF. In this deadly concert, the overloaded chopper, unlike a *Valkyrie* of lore, did not bear the men off to *Valhalla*, but was hit by ground fire and landed with an unceremonial thud on the street below. The iron–nerved aviator maneuvered it down the street like a taxi and pulled into a parking lot. Using several tall apartment buildings as a shield, the pilot again tried to make his getaway but the Little Bird was knocked down again, this time for good, and the men formed a defensive perimeter nearby. Seconds after one DELTA trooper held up an infrared strobe light, they were spotted by a Black Hawk, and the cavalry came to the rescue in the form of three 6th Infantry Regiment M-113 armored personnel carriers. Four DELTA troopers were hurt, one seriously, but unlike the events some nine years earlier in Iran, this plan was carried out and with the intended results.

(**Top**) The MH-6J Little Bird that lifted Kurt Muse to freedom is moved out of the street by US mechanized forces after they secured the area around General Manuel Noriega's headquarters. Note the three–man troop seats along each side and the large crane–like appendage for fast –rope operations. It folds forward against the side of the bird when not in use and inadvertently prevents troopers from easily exiting the interior from the right side. (**Right**) The battered *Comandancia*, located just across the street from Muse's prison cell. *Soldier of Fortune*

Air Support

Rotary– and Fixed–Wing Assets

The Holloway Report on Operation *Eagle Claw* laid bare the grevious deficiencies in special operations aviation that contributed to the disaster at *Desert I*; chief among them was the lack of interoperability between the armed services. The conglomeration of hardware fielded by special operations aviation was the most visible manifestation of this shortcoming.

Throughout the early 1980s, special operations aviation soldiered on with an unwieldy mix of helicopters. Depending on the mission (and what was available), a DELTA trooper might easily find himself working with CH-3 Jolly Green Giants, CH-53C Sea Stallions, UH1–1N Twin Hueys, CH-47D Chinooks, some newer (and extensively modified) UH-60A Black Hawks, HH-53B and C Pave Low IIIs, and substantially upgraded versions of the OH-6A Cayuse called AH and MH-6 "Little Birds." One highly capable helicopter that DELTA

could *not* count on using, except, perhaps, in the most extreme emergency, was the RH-53Ds of *Eagle Claw*. The Navy's entire fleet of this counter–mine version of the Sea Stallion amounted to only twenty–four aircraft before a half–dozen were lost in the Dasht–e Kavir, severely degrading the fleet's mine–sweeping capability. They had been tapped for the mission because the stretched HH-53s, specifically designed for special ops, were literally too long to fit in the elevators of most aircraft carriers without time–consuming removal of their rotor blades, a problem that persists today, even though many of the vessels with smaller elevators have been retired.

Members of all armed services found themselves in general agreement with the Holloway Report's findings, and some organizational, equipment, and training improvements were made. But the most basic problem remained: the lack of "jointness" be-

A Pave Low jockey wearing AN/PVS-5A night vision goggles. Even relatively lightweight goggles require that a counterweight be attached to the back of a pilot's helmet, and after a year of night flying an airman's collar size often increases a size or two from the increased exercise of his neck muscles.

tween the Army, Navy, Marines, and Air Force. Under pressure from congress, the Department of Defense attempted, unsuccessfully, to put an end to the interservice rivalries by advocating that the Army become the sole operator of rotary–wing special operations assets, while the Air Force continued to develop its long–range, fixed–wing capability.

Although this particular proposal went nowhere fast because of both congressional backpedaling and continued resistance within the Air Force to anything that would cut into its turf, the future security of the nation was immeasurably enhanced by passage of the 1987 Defense Authorization Act, which established a unified command incorporating the special operations forces from all services. The new Special Operations Command (SOCOM) could train and deploy forces throughout the world and was given the authority to develop and acquire equipment, services, and supplies peculiar to special ops. Of particular interest to DELTA, was the funding and authorization to modify existing aircraft and develop new helicopter variants.

Under the act, the UH-60 Black Hawk would be reconfigured into three basic models to support all services. The Army's 160th Special Operations Aviation Regiment, Airborns (SOAR) would use the MH-60K Pave Hawk to replace its less–capable MH-60As* in the assault role; the HH-60H "Rescue

*The L variant Black Hawks, with their more–powerful engines, uprated transmissions, and HIRSS (Hover Infrared Supression Subsystem) would not enter service till the following year, 1988. All MH-60As and many UH-60As have since been retrofitted with the HIRSS.

(**Above**) The aftermath of an unscheduled Pave Low landing in Korea. No one was injured in the accident which occurred during a night training exercise. (**Opposite**) HC-130 Combat Shadow tankers and MH-53 Pave Low helicopters.

Hawk" would enhance the Navy's search and rescue as well as special warfare capability; and the Air Force MH-60G Pave Hawk would both replace its aging search and rescue aircraft as well as act as an armed escort for the new MH-53J Pave Low IIIs just entering service. All aircraft would be provided with tiedowns to allow shipboard operations.

The newest Pave Low III variant of the CH-53, called the MH-53J, was tasked to perform the heavy–lift, rotary–wing effort for the near future. A superb special ops aircraft, it is, unfortunately, rather short–legged, and even with the addition of a 600gal fuel bladder, it requires frequent air refuel-

ing during long missions. Congressional sponsors of the 1987 legislation—as well as the Air Force hierarchy—envisioned that it would be phased out of special operations and into search and rescue as MH-47Es came on line.

The special operations variant of the venerable, heavy–lift CH-47D Chinook would complement the MH-60K's mission. Unlike the Pave Low IIIs, MH-47Es can easily fit into the elevators of all aircraft carriers and, thus, offers planners more deployment options. The MH-47E would also have an interoperable avionics system with its smaller cousin and could engage in full and open competition with the CV-22A Osprey for the long–range strategic special ops mission. Unfortunately, the extremely versatile tilt–rotor Osprey, which incorporated the lift, range and speed of a fixed–wing transport with the vertical–lift capability of a helicopter, was canceled by the Defense Department during the post–Cold War budget cuts.

Unlike other special ops helicopters, the AH and MH-6 Little Birds are not dealt with in the published versions of congressional defense appropriations. These descendants of the trusty old Cayuse were developd and fielded through the use of covert funds in much the same way as the F-117 stealth attack aircraft and, interestingly, started to edge out of the "black" at approximately the same time as the the F-117, primarily because of their high visibility during the 1987–1988 retaliatory attacks on Iranian targets in the Persian Gulf and the 1989 overthrow of Panamanian dictator Manuel Noriega.

The 160th SOAR, which carried out these operations, is known as the Night Stalkers, because of their effective use of darkness during missions, and many of its pilots have logged 2,000 or more flight hours wearing night vision goggles. The regiment, headquartered at Fort Campbell, Kentucky, is composed of four battalions: the 1st with eighteen AH-6s, eighteen MH-6s and thirty MH-60 (incorporating the forward–deployed 617th Special Operations Aviation Detachment (Airborne) in Panama); the 2d with twenty–four MH-47s; the 3d with ten MH-60s and eight MH-47s, based at Hunter Army Airfield, Savannah, Georgia, to support the 1st Ranger Battalion, as it did during the Grenada operation; and an Oklahoma National Guard battalion, the 1/245, based at Tulsa, Oklahoma, with more than three dozen aircraft including fifteen UH-60Ls which will eventually be replaced by MH-60s.

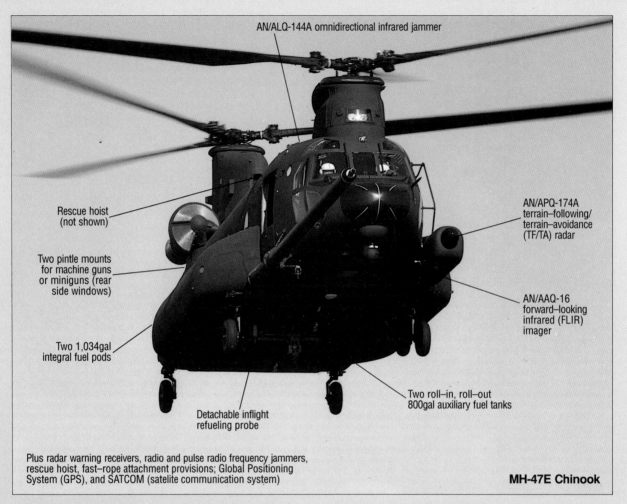

AN/ALQ-144A omnidirectional infrared jammer

Rescue hoist
(not shown)

Two pintle mounts
for machine guns
or miniguns (rear
side windows)

Two 1,034gal
integral fuel pods

Detachable inflight
refueling probe

AN/APQ-174A
terrain–following/
terrain–avoidance
(TF/TA) radar

AN/AAQ-16
forward–looking
infrared (FLIR)
imager

Two roll–in, roll–out
800gal auxiliary fuel tanks

Plus radar warning receivers, radio and pulse radio frequency jammers,
rescue hoist, fast–rope attachment provisions; Global Positioning
System (GPS), and SATCOM (satelite communication system)

MH-47E Chinook

MH-47E Chinook and
MH-60 Black Hawk Variants

(**Above**) The MH-47E's highly advanced, integrated avionics system and extended range allow it to complete clandestine, deep–penetration missions. The aircraft can easily use nap–of–the–earth tactics at night and in any weather conditions while placing a minimum workload on the pilot. Special operations enhanced UH-60 Black Hawks have performed spectacularly in long–range combat operations from Grenada to Iraq. (**Opposite top**) An MH-60 Enhanced Black Hawk (sometimes referred to as a Pave Hawk) of the Army's 160th SOAR named *Executioner*, upgraded from either an UH-60A or L. (**Opposite center**) A newly built MH-60G Pave Hawk undergoing flight testing. (**Opposite bottom**) An Air Force MH-60K Pave Hawk upgraded from a UH-60A. All of these helicopters wear infrared–suppressing paint.

MH-60 Enhanced Black Hawk

Two pintle mounts for machine guns or miniguns (forward side windows)

AN/ALQ-144 omnidirectional infrared jammer

Hover infrared suppression subsystem (HIRSS)

AN/AAQ-16 FLIR imager

Two 7.62mm miniguns

Two nineteen–round 70mm rockets launchers

M-130 flare/chaff dispenser tied to missile detector

Plus radar warning receiver, rescue hoist, fast–rope attachment provisions, GPS, and SATCOM

MH-60G Pave Hawk

Wire strike protection

Two pintle mounts for machine guns or miniguns (forward side windows)

AN/AAQ-16 FLIR imager

Inflight refueling probe

AN/APN-239 weather radar (with ground mapping modes)

M-130 flare/chaff dispenser tied to missile detector (will be replaced by ALE-40 dispensers)

Plus radar warning receiver, radio and pulse radio frequency jammers, rescue hoist, fast–rope rappelling system, GPS and SATCOM

MH-60K Pave Hawk

AN/ALQ-144A omnidirectional infrared jammer

Wire strike protection

HIRSS

M–130 flare/chaff dispensertied to missile detector

Two crash–worthy 230gal external auxiliary fuel tanks

AN/APQ-174A TF/TA radar

Inflight refueling probe

AN/AAQ-16 FLIR imager

Two pintle mounts for machine guns or miniguns

Mounts for air–to–air or air–to–ground rockets

Plus radar warning receivers, radio and pulse radio frequency jammers, rescue hoist, fast rope rappelling system, GPS, SATCOM, and laser detector

Close–ups of .50cal machine gun (**top**) and 7.62mm minigun (**above**) on pintle mounts bolted to Pave Low III ramp decks.

GPS antenna

Two rear AN/ALQ-162 electronic countermeasures (ECM) antennas

600gal internal auxiliary fuel bladder

Pintle mount for machine gun or minigun (ramp)

Rescue hoist

Two crash–worthy 650gal external auxiliary fuel tanks

Two AN/ALQ-157(V)2 infrared countermeasures jammers on outrigger pylons

Two pintle mounts for machine guns or miniguns (forward side windows)

Two forward AN/ALQ-162 ECM antennas

AN/ALR-69(V)6 radar warning receiver

Retractable inflight refueling probe

AN/APQ-158(V)2 Tf/TA radar

AN/AAQ-10 FLIR imager

Infrared searchlight

MH-53J Pave Low III (enhanced)

Plus fast–rope rappelling system, flare/chaff dispensers and SATCOM

MH-53
Pave Low III

The MH-53H and J Pave Low IIIs are descended from a long line of Sikorsky helicopters that have performed rescue and special operations from the Korean War through Vietnam and the aborted 1980 raid to free American hostages in Iran. Of a family that is second only to the Soviet–built Mi-26 Halo in size and heavy–lift capability, the Pave Low III is capable of operating with pin–point accuracy in all weather conditions and at night. It also shares many components with other Air Force assets, such as the FLIR on the AC-130 Specter gunships and MC-130 Combat Talons transports. **(Top)** Special operations forces exit the rear of a Pave Low III via a flexable ladder and **(above)** by fast–rope. **(Opposite)** An MH-53J skimming the trees. One recent night training exercise included seven Pave Lows receiving four inflight refuelings each during a nearly eight–hour flight. The exercise concluded with the helicopters arriving within two seconds of their target time and unloading thirty men each in five seconds.

MD 530MG

Little Bird Variants

Based on an extremely popular airframe that can be found in extensive use by both civilian and government entities in every corner of the globe, the Little Bird offers great agility, adaptability, and its own version of visual stealth if such is warranted by a mission. The aircraft is manufactured by McDonnell Douglas and carries a basic civilian designation of either MD 500 or MD 530. The 500, 500C, and 500D aircraft were produced with a round, bubble–like nose through 1982 when all subsequent helicopters of these types were manufactured with

the more pointed nose of the MD 500E, 500F, and 500MG, as well as the slightly larger and more powerful MD 520 and 530 series aircraft. The US Army's orders for these helicopters after 1982, however, have generally called for the retention of the bubble nose to maintain the option of installing a TOW antitank missile aiming sight and keep visual commonality with the large number of pre–1982, nonmilitary aircraft of this type.

The high civilian and foreign–military demand for a small, reliable, inexpensive helicopter was coupled with the manufacturer's effort to fill that demand by incorporating a large variety of powerplant, transmission, rotor, and other changes on what is essentially the same airframe. This proliferation of different aircraft types found its way into the 160th SOAR's inventory since there was never a specific production line opened for the US Army, all purchases being made in bits and pieces over a decade of off–the–shelf buying to supplement its original OH-6A Cayuse helicopters. This proliferation has led to a mind–boggling alphabet soup of aircraft types in the 160th's 1st Battalion, the unit that most directly supports DELTA. Jane's *All the World's Aircraft* states that the MH-6B and AH-6C are derived from the OH-6A; the AH-6F and MH-6E from MD 500MG; and the AH-6G, MH-6F and MH-6J from the MD 530MG. "A" designations are given to the heavily armed attack versions of the Little Bird, which can be armed with a variety of miniguns, machine guns, rockets, and missiles. Nearly all Little Birds are equipped with a swinging, crane–like arm for fast–rope rappeling and Stabo operations, and the AH-6G, MH-6E, MH-6F, and possibly the AH-6F, have multifunction displays and forward–looking infrared (FLIR) imagers to be used in association with night vision goggles.

(**Opposite**) MD 530MG unleashing a salvo of 70mm rockets during weapons testing at the US Army's Yuma Proving Grounds, Arizona and closeups of seven–tube 70mm rocket launcher and TOW antitank missile pod. (**Top to bottom**) 160th SOAR AH-6G Little Bird bereft of any identifying markings or "sterile"; an MD 530N equipped with NOTAR (no tail rotor) system, including close–up of steering louvres on underside of tail; and MD 530N configured for transportation with louver cone and tail fins folded upward and main rotor blades stowed along tail boom. Note that the MD 530 models in the lower photos have both the pointed nose, for streamlining, and the pre–1982 bubble nose of the MD 500 series aircraft still used on most military variants.

Of great benefit to DELTA in urban counterterrorist situations is the 160th SOAR's conversion to the NOTAR system on its Little Birds. The NOTAR uses a variable–pitch fan and direct jet thruster to push cool air through longitudinal steering louvres on a circulation control tailboom. Although early tests by the 160th showed "higher than desired pilot workload" due to a tendency for the nose to wander at low speeds, yaw–only stability augmentation corrected the problem. With the NOTAR system, AH/MH-6 aircraft display a greatly reduced acoustic signature, increased hover stability, and roughly double the lateral and rearward speeds of conventional helicopters. The absence of a tail rotor also eliminates the danger of tail strikes on ground crew and allows DELTA troopers more freedom of movement around the aircraft during operations.

AN/ALQ-144A omnidirectional infrared jammer

Two seven–tube 70mm rocket launchers

AN/AAQ-16 FLIR imager

AH-6G

MD 530N

MD 530N

AC-130 Specter Gunship

The AC-130 Specter gunship is a basic C-130 modified with side–mounted weapons and various sensors that make it highly adaptable to a variety of special missions. When fielded against targets with few antiaircraft defenses and a minimal air threat, the Specter is able to provide close air support much more efficiently than a large force of fighter aircraft and is a particularly effective platform for interdiction and armed reconnaissance missions. The Specter has the ability to aid in perimeter defense, escort, surveillance, search and rescue, infiltration/exfiltration, illumination, and landing zone support operations, as well as to conduct limited airborne command and control functions for other strike aircraft.

The AC-130H is armed with two 20mm Gatling–type guns, a rapid–firing 40mm cannon and 105mm howitzer supported by a laser rangefinder (which can also be used for marking targets for laser–guided bombs), an infrared sensor to identify heat sources such as people and vehicles, a beacon–tracking radar, a fire control computer, two–kilowatt searchlight and a low–light–level television capable of amplifying even faint traces of starlight to monitor both targets and friendly forces. The newer AC-130U models have retained the 40 and 105mm weapons but use a single 25mm Gatling–type gun fed by a two–canister, automated loading system instead of the H models' 20mm guns which required their linked ammunition to

be hand–loaded. Other new features have also been added such as the F-15's fire control radar, lightweight Kevlar armor, inflight refueling capability, and a highly efficient, soundproof battle management center.

Depending on the type of target, threat environment, weather, and desired level of destruction, weapons can be accurately employed at altitudes from 3,000 to 20,000 feet above ground level. The Specter fires from a constant angle of bank and, at a typical slant range of 10,000 feet, the remarkably stable gun platform can deliver ordnance within ten feet of its target even under conditions of low cloud ceilings or poor visibility. Unlike fighter aircraft, which must make separate runs on hostile forces, targets are continually visible throughout the gunship's entire orbit and can be fired on at will. But even though the run–in headings required by fighter aircraft are not needed, no–fire headings may be imposed from the ground or automatically computed by the aircrew if there is a risk of short rounds hitting friendly forces from a particular angle.

The Specter's two–kilowatt searchlight can be used to illuminate targets and landing zones, aid in search and rescue, and supply light for the television sensor if its illuminator is inoperative. In combat, the searchlight is normally used in a covert infrared mode, to provide illumination for night vision devices, since its overt white light mode would easily pinpoint the gunship's position for hostile forces. Its effectiveness is reduced with altitude and weather.

DELTA troopers in a tight spot can mark their ground position with a wide variety of items. First, Mk-6 and Mk-25 ground markers can be dropped by hand from the rear of the Specter, itself, and will burn for forty–five and thirty minutes, respectively. Next, transponders, including the handheld SST-101 miniponder, can be picked up by the aircraft's beacon tracking radar at up to ten nautical miles and the powerful AN/UPN-25 and SST-181x transponders can be received by the ship's navigation radar at up to sixty nautical miles. A standard survival vest strobe light with a removeable infrared filter can also be used either visually or with the filter installed. The infrared filter provides the same information to the aircrew as the unmasked strobe but prevents visible light from revealing the friendly ground position

to the enemy forces. Positive identification is provided by turning one or more strobes off and on in response to radio instructions for the aircrew. The old standby, lightweight three–by–five–foot cloth reflective panels, can clearly mark ground reference points when illuminated by the Specter, either overtly or covertly. Other methods of marking positions include flashlights, vehicle lights, pen gun flares, tracer rounds, fires, fire arrows, signal mirrors, and simply running a vehicle engine with the ignition unshielded.

(**Opposite**) An AC-130H Specter fires its 105mm gun during a night exercise; (**top**) airmen loading a Specter's 40mm gun; (**left**) twin 20mm Gatling–type guns aft of the cockpit; and (**right**) 40mm and 105mm guns forward of the aircraft's loading ramp.

89

MC-130 Combat Talon and HC-130 Combat Shadow

The mission of the MC-130E and H Combat Talons is to conduct day and night infiltration, exfiltration, resupply, psychological operations, and aerial reconnaissance into hostile or enemy controlled territory using air landings, air drops or surface–to–air recoveries. The use of FLIR imagers enables aircrews to visually identify targets and checkpoints at night while terrain–following/terrain–avoidance(TF/TA) radar and an inertial navigation system allow extreme accuracy while navigating to unmarked drop zones. Missions are normally flown at night using a high–low–high altitude profile. The high portion is flown prior to penetrating and after exiting the target area at an altitude that minimizes fuel consumption and enemy detection. The aircraft then descends to the lowest possible altitude consistent with flying safety and uses its TF/TA radar to penetrate and operate in hostile territory.

The Talon's range depends on several factors, including configuration, payload, en route winds and weather, and the length of time spent at fuel–guzzling, low–level flight. For planning purposes, its range (without refueling and factoring in two hours at low level) is 2,800 nautical miles. With inflight refueling, the Talon's range is limited only by the availability of tanker support and the effect

that crew fatigue may have on the mission. The Talon is not a rapid response aircraft. Operating deep in heavily defended enemy territory requires extensive preflight planning, and units normally receive notification at least forty–eight hours out with a final briefing on threats and positions of friendly forces before takeoff.

Aircrews are capable of successfully operating at unmarked drop zones (DZs) but usually have something they can hang their headphones on. When ground and air component commanders agree to use a specific DZ, reception committee personnel coordinate with the aircrew on the type of markings to be used, configuration of the DZ, method of authentication and release point determination. The most frequent cause for mission aborts is a lack of coordination or confusion over marking procedures; it is important to note that terrain–following is made difficult during moderate showers and even further degraded during heavy thunderstorms.

Depending on mission, an aircrew makes either a static–line, low–altitude air drop; a high–altitude, low–opening (HALO) air drop; a surface–to–air recovery (STAR) using a Fulton extraction system; or may simply land the aircraft. For static–line drops during combat operations, a Talon is flown as low as 750 feet while a HALO drop, which requires a free fall before parachute opening, is never conducted from lower than 1,500 feet. For static–line drops combining both men and equipment (such as rubber rafts), troops exit immediately after ejection of equipment. A STAR can be used for the extractions during either day or night but requires fairly good weather to accomplish the mission safely. Either two people or 500 pounds of equipment can be picked up over land or water per pass. During air landings, the minimum length necessary is the takeoff/landing roll plus 500 feet for a total of approximately 3,000 feet. The Talon's minimum required runway width is sixty feet and, while the capability exists to set down at a landing zone that has no lights or is lit with infrared lights, use of the Special Forces seven–light panel marking system (which includes a 250–foot/ten percent safety zone at each end out) is preferred.

The HC-130P Combat Shadow tankers have essentially the same extensive radar and navigational aids as the Combat Talon, as well as the ability to refuel two helicopters simultaneously in flight. After the tanker unreels its fuel line and slows to approximately 120mph, the Shadow's customer slowly edges its refuel probe closer to the drogue–tipped hose while making certain that it stays beneath or to the outside of the tankers turbulent slipstream. It generally takes an MH-53 less than ten minutes to top off and an MH-47, with its huge fuel blisters, can get its fill in about fifteen minutes.

(Opposite) The retracted nose prongs, which, when extended forward and out, snag the line of a target balloon during surface–to–air recoveries, can be clearly seen in this shot of a MC-130 receiving fuel from a KC-135 tanker. See page 120 for a complete recovery sequence. (Top left) A Vietnam–era MC-130 rigged for a pick–up with guard cables running from the top of its bulbous nose to its wingtips and (top right) a similarly configured MC-130E or H variant. Note the difference in radar bulge configuration on the newer aircraft, to accommodate its expanded TF/TA, FLIR, and other systems, as well as its lengthened prongs. (Above left) TF/TA radar screen, displaying an obstruction in the aircraft's path as a blob below the upwardly bowed line, and a portion of the FLIR display off to the left. These systems and all other internal controls can be made to glow in a subdued mode so that they do not interfere with the pilot's night vision goggles. (Above right) An MH-60 carefully maneuvering its refuel probe up to an HC-130's extended fuel line and drogue.

Chapter 5
Back to the Desert

The deep sleep of the early morning hours was interrupted by the familiar obnoxious sound of a pager going off. Reaching for his clothing, the young Sergeant kissed his wife's head and ambled down the hall to check on his son. Allowing the hall light to play over the boy's sandy hair, the trooper bent down to kiss him goodbye as he had so often in the past. Waiting until he had left the house, he sat on the front steps to pull on his well worn cowboy boots. He climbed into his pickup truck and drove to the post. In less than two hours, the young sergeant's troop was winging away from Pope Air Force Base near Fort Bragg. As the wheels of the lumbering C-141 Starlifter retracted into their wells, his troop commander was already scanning the initial intelligence reports from the agencies supporting the unit. Things were not so good in the land of oil and sand.

At 0400 on the morning of Thursday, August 2, 1990, mechanized elements of Saddam Hussein's elite Republican Guards stabbed across the desert frontier separating Iraq and Kuwait east of the disputed Rumalia oilfield. Iraqi forces had been massing steadily across the border for almost two weeks before the invasion, but both Western and Arabian governments believed this to be nothing more than a show of force to bolster Saddam's financial claims against the oil-rich kingdom. By midday, all meaningful resistance by Kuwait's tiny army had been crushed and its royal family had fled to a sumptuous exile in Saudi Arabia.

The Baathist government in Baghdad rejoiced

A thirsty trooper inhales bottled water in the shade of a C-141 StarLifter in Saudi Arabia.

over its quick victory and believed that it had been accomplished with such speed that the world was presented with a *fait accompli*. Saddam expected a toothless condemnation from the United Nations and perhaps even a half–hearted economic embargo that would soon fade away. But his analysis was fatally flawed. US and British leaders meeting in the United States immediately resolved that the rest of the Middle East's oil resources must be kept out of Saddam's bloodied hands, at all costs. Even before his generals gathered their forces for the next morning's move to the Saudi border, numerous elements of America's special operations forces were either already deployed or were going "wheels up" from bases in the United States and Europe.

From the first moment President George Bush was notified that Iraqi forces were plunging across

Kuwait's border, one of the prime challenges to face him as the National Command Authority was the possibility—indeed probability—that large numbers of Americans would become prisoners in a dangerous diplomatic game. The specter of a second major Middle East hostage crisis loomed over the Pentagon and the White House. Although public speculation was kept to a minimum, no one needed to be reminded that the Carter administration fell because of the prolonged hostage crisis in Iran. The extreme vulnerability of the US Embassy staff and numerous Americans associated with Kuwait's petroleum industry was evident. When coupled with the Baathist regime's close ties with terrorist groups, history of wanton aggression against its neighbors, and deadly abuse of its own people, the president had no choice but to act. Although special operations forces assets already in the Gulf were capable of performing the hasty option response, the National Command Authority launched the first DELTA assets into the Middle East.

Crisis action teams were dispatched to Saudi Arabia and other friendly nations to establish C^3 (command, control, and communications) sites for future operations and to provide a terminal for information to and from Washington. Launch sites for missions were identified and staging areas hastily opened. Meanwhile, back at Fort Bragg, the Joint Special Operations Command (JSOC) worked hard to avoid being caught flatfooted and began building a massive workup of target folders for the "long war" that was sure to come.

Other important assets moving into the area were elements of the Intelligence Support Activity (ISA). Like so many other parts of the special operations force, ISA was an offshoot of the Desert I afteraction review. A critical failing during the hostage crisis in Iran was the lack of information from human intelligence sources or HUMINT. In Iran, DELTA did not have an "eyeball" on its target. In Iraq and Kuwait, ISA would provide the needed eyes.

Various elements of the myriad special operations units in Europe and the United States continued to trickle in, and most of the burden of working with the resistance inside Kuwait was assumed by the Special Forces units that already had that mission in accordance with theater war plans. As predicted, US and other foreign nationals did indeed become "guests" at selected Iraqi strategic military and nuclear sites but were eventually allowed to leave as a "gesture of goodwill" when their continued captivity threatened to precipitate, not prevent, an assault on Iraq. DELTA remained.

Commencement of the coalition air campaign raised fears that hostages might be taken in retaliation at widely scattered locations around the globe, and additional target folders of possible hostage-holding centers began to take shape. While significant terrorist operations never emerged, the public display of Allied prisoners of war did cause concern at the highest levels, and plans were formulated to rescue those individuals. Small teams were also selected to carry out a number of sensitive, direct-action missions against targets in Iraq's command and control nets.

Initially, special operations units were faced with the same problem they have always had to deal with: How to get the conventional force commanders to use their capabilities properly or even at all. For example, the 75th Ranger Regiment's assessment team left the Gulf after finding out that there was very little they could do in the theater, and the elite light infantry of the 82d Airborne Division was severely handicapped on the billiard table–terrain without an immense amount of support.

Colonel Jessie Johnson, commander of Central Command's (CENTCOM's) Special Operations Command (SOC), drafted his campaign plans for the upcoming desert war from his headquarters at King Fahd International Airport near Dhahran. A

(**Right**) All–terrain Fast Attack Vehicles (FAVs) and motorcycles (**above**) saw extensive use by special operations forces, including DELTA, during operations in Iraq and Kuwait and operated from forward bases in Saudi Arabia or base camps established far behind Iraqi lines. Motorcycles with heavily muffled engines offered troopers individualized, high–speed movement coupled with the ability to approach a target from several axes simultaneously and, on some types of missions, would be used in combination with FAVs.

Capable of being armed with a wide assortment of goodies—machine guns, antitank weapons, grenade launchers and almost anything else one might think of—FAVs offered substantial hitting power and the ability to travel extended distances across the desert at speeds up to 80– plus mph. The vehicles pictured here both mount AT4 antitank missile launchers on the outsides of their frame roofs and M60E3 machine guns forward of the passenger seats. An additional gunner sits in the elevated, rear seat, which can swivel around for firing at targets behind the vehicle. In the top photo, this position mounts a .50cal machine gun while the vehicle above sports a 40mm grenade launcher. Note the dart board taped to the nose of the FAV at lower left, a not–so–subtle comment by its crew on their vulnerability. *Soldier of Fortune*.

veteran of *Desert I*, where he commanded the joint Ranger–DELTA road–watch teams, Johnson knew what difficulties awaited his forces. Luckily for him, his boss at CENTCOM, General H. Norman Schwarzkopf, had the utmost confidence in his special ops commander. Despite attempts by elements within the Joint Chiefs of Staff, to replace him with a two–star officer, Schwarzkopf kept his faith in Johnson, who in return, became the architect for several brilliantly executed operations.

Saddam's Vengence Weapon

As the war progressed, another in history's long line of terror weapons was unleashed in the Middle East: the Scud B medium–range ballistic missile, successor to Hitler's infamous V-1 and V-2 rockets

DELTA operated out of secure, remote bases dotting the desert wastes south of the Saudi–Iraqi border. **(Above)** A C-130, of unidentified type, sits baking under "big red" across from a special operations Black Hawk with external, add–on fuel tanks. **(Left)** Air base security armed for bear with a combination M16 assault rifle/M203 grenade launcher. His vest is packed with twenty 40mm grenades for the M203, and he is using night vision goggles, which turn even the blackest nights into a green day, to scan the perimeter.

broadcasts gleefully warned Britons of the immense destruction that would be wreaked on their cities by the "vengeance" weapons. Since their target was an English–speaking public, the Nazis named their rockets the V-1 and V-2, instead of giving them an "R" designation for the equivalent German word, *rache*.

The Scud retained many of the V-2's basic characteristics, along with many deadly improvements. Highly mobile, it nevertheless required more than an hour to fuel and its involved targeting procedures took excruciatingly long to complete, even when performed by experienced crews at preplotted sites. To make matters even more interesting, homemade

of World War II. On those earlier weapons, The "V" designation was, itself, part of Hitler's psychological warfare campaign aimed at terrorizing the British people. Nazi English–language propaganda

(**Right**) A Scud B medium–range ballistic missile on its MAZ-543 transporter–erector–launcher and (**above**) a rare photograph of a Scud impact. Even before certain changes were made to the weapon that degraded its accuracy, it was not known for its ability to make pinpoint strikes. The weapon in the above photo was fired by Soviet forces at Afghan guerrillas who had surrounded Loyalist troops at an isolated garrison. It missed the guerrillas and instead landed within the government troops' defensive perimeter. Above: *Soldier of Fortune*.

versions of the missile, like the *al Hussein*, incorporated range enhancements that both reduced its warhead capacity and severely degraded its ability to strike near its target.

The Soviets designed the Scud to deliver small nuclear warheads, or as an area saturation system when fired in conventional battery salvos; the Iraqis instead used it as simply a fire–in–the–general–direction–of–your–adversary–and–then–wait–for–the–results weapon. Fixed launch sites containing both real and dummy missiles existed at airfields in western Iraq, targeting Israel, and in eastern Iraq, aimed at Iran and Saudi Arabia. These sites were well known to US and Israeli planners and could be easily removed from the picture. It was Saddam's surprisingly large number of wheeled launchers for the Scud and shorter–range Frog missiles that proved to be exceedingly difficult targets for air reconnaissance assets to locate. This difficulty in targeting the mobile launchers in the wide expanses of Iraq set the stage for one role the troopers of DELTA never dreamed of or trained for: Scud hunting.

The scenario thrust upon DELTA was a far cry from the world of takedowns and hostage rescues each man became immersed in the moment he entered Wally World. Many, if not all, the troops deployed to the Gulf had extensive training in their initial Special Forces specialties and were already experts in carrying out such standard missions as unconventional warfare, special reconnaissance, foreign internal defense, plus search and rescue operations, to name just a few, but it was the introduction of Saddam's terror weapons that forced the counterterrorists to revert to these basic war–fighting specialties and become what the press dubbed "super commandos." Curiously enough, though, since Scud missiles served no real military purpose —when used as they were by the Iraqis— DELTA troopers could still be said to be involved in a new, unanticipated form of counterterrorism.

The war was going poorly for the Iraqi warlord, and he knew that his best bet to overcome the military setbacks around was to drive a wedge between the Arab and Western elements in the coalition arrayed against him. If attacks on Jewish population centers could push Israel into a knee–jerk military response, Saddam believed that indignant Arab masses would finally heed his call for a *jihad*, or holy war, and either overthrow unfriendly governments like President Hosni Mubarak's in Egypt or, at the very least, force their governments to withdraw from the coalition. Western elements isolated at the end of a very long logistics line would be forced into an ignominious withdrawal.

Saddam's strategy was not difficult to anticipate, and the White House made it crystal clear through strong public statements (coupled with a rapid, showy deployment of a Patriot surface–to–air missile battery to Tel Aviv) that the drawing of Israel into the war would be prevented at all costs. CENTCOM had no choice but to commit its Air Force component to a resource–consuming search for mobile launchers with little to show for its efforts.* This same mission was also handed to the Army's Special Forces, who, if necessary, would actually target individual vehicles for air strikes— an extremely risky business for the troops involved but a mission that was, in light of the strategic situation, of immense importance. CENTCOM quickly discovered, however, that a critical shortage of trained special recon teams existed in the Kuwaiti Theater of Operations (KTO).

Every available Green Beret was committed to serving as liaison with the Saudi Army, training Kuwaiti resistance forces, or conducting intelligence–gathering missions for General Schwarzkopf's headquarters. When it became necessary to scrape together additional assets to help locate Scuds, the only force in the KTO was the counterterrorists of DELTA, as well as some British SAS personnel. Reports by the European and American news media later referred to this use of DELTA as if the unit were some sort of key reserve, when, in reality, it was all Schwarzkopf had at the moment.

Special operations assets made available by the coalition forces, primarily DELTA and the desert–wise SAS, were formed into teams and prepared for the upcoming operations.* At first, though, Colonel

*The continued success of the Iraqis at hitting Israeli and Saudi population centers necessitated that a full squadron of F-15Es be essentially pulled from the air campaign and assigned the task of eliminating mobile Scuds. Other air assets were soon added as the equivalent of three squadrons became tied up by the effort, and the number of sorties by Scud–hunting intelligence, refueling and strike aircraft sometimes climbed to more than 300 per twenty–four hour period. Although a severe drain on US resources, this heavy and prolonged commitment was instrumental in convincing the Israelis to call off two planned raids into western Iraq that could have had a disastrous effect on the war effort.

Johnson's professionals from Smoke Bomb Hill and the Ranch were understandably missing from the almost–continuous Gulf news coverage, while other forces from Fort Bragg, the XVIIIth Airborne Corps, 1st Corps Support Command, and the renowned 82d Airborne Division received their share of the limelight. But it wasn't long before reporters were hearing strange tales of parachutes gliding silently through the Arabian night to deposit their human cargo on the desert floor. The stories are many, but all have the same theme and similar scenarios. The following is just one of them. Maybe it's just a good piece of propaganda; then again, maybe it's true.

Prepping the Battlefield

An in-depth mission analysis was conducted on the upcoming Scud hunt by the intelligence agencies supporting the theater's special operations forces. The intel experts looked at such subjects as the terrain and infiltration/exfiltration routes

---
*The SAS not only retains a great deal of institutional knowledge on desert warfare but also makes frequent use of a training area in the Gulf state of Oman.

US special operations forces did not truly "own the night" as the often–repeated slogan claimed, but did operate extremely effectively in that environment, due to a combination of superb training and equipment. (**Above** and **above right**) Troopers viewed through a NVG move out under cover of darkness and rappel from a Black Hawk.

---

through Iraqi antiaircraft belts and known locations of enemy units were plotted on the situation maps. As this information was analyzed, a clear picture emerged indicating that the majority of the target areas could be easily reached by Army MH-60 Pave Hawks of the 160th Special Operations Aviation Regiment (Airborne) or Air Force MH-53 Pave Low IIIs of the 1st Special Operations Wing.

Unfortunately, the extremely heavy demand for the specialized helicopters in the KTO, as well as various other considerations, meant that they could not be used in every situation. For tactical reasons, it was decided that the target area around which this story centers necessitated that DELTA conduct a HAHO infiltration. HAHO (pronounced *hey–ho*)

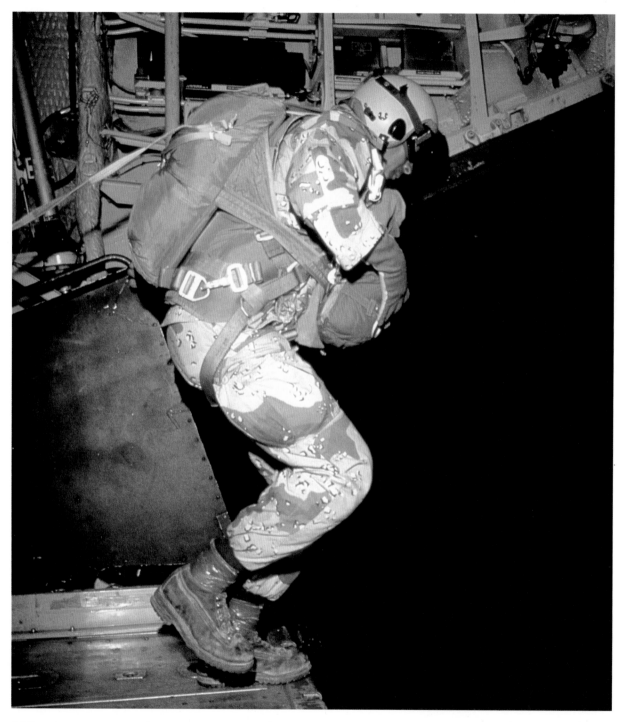

is the acronym for high–altitude, high–opening and essentially means that the drop is conducted at about 30,000 feet or higher, with the jumper opening his parachute almost immediately after clearing the plane. The trooper then glides his maneuverable, double–canopy parachute through the sky and lands with pinpoint accuracy at a predetermined site. The distance from the point that the jumper pulls his rip cord and where he lands can be as much as fifty miles.

The team participating in this unique Scud–hunting mission is required to prepare a "briefback" on how each trooper will carry out his duties. The briefback is standard operating procedure within the special operations community and covers the friendly versus enemy situation, the mission, its execution, support requirements, command structures, and a short, concise, yet detailed narrative of how the trooper will help accomplish the mission. The briefback is normally given to the leadership of the unit and not only demonstrates to the commander that his men are ready, but also assures the team that everyone is playing off the same sheet of music.

After a few carefully considered questions, the team is given the go–ahead and conducts final rehearsals, equipment checks, and other preparations. On this mission, they are more concerned with the "sneak and peek" than direct–action aspects of the operation. If they can find the missile's elusive transporter–erector–launchers (TELs), they will call

An Air Force Special Operations combat control team member exits from the open ramp of a MC–130 Combat Talon. Control teams are often inserted before the arrival of special operations or conventional forces to mark landing or drop zones that must be used at night by pilots using NVGs and arcraft fitted with infrared imagers. For example, a control team member had already arrived at and marked the *Desert I* refuel site in Iran before the arrival of the aircraft bearing DELTA. The lack of weapon and rucksack indicates that this was taken during a practice exercise.

in an air strike and, if circumstances require it, use a portable laser to target the weapon for destruction by the fast–movers of the Air Force.

The basic plan is simple. The team will move undetected from their drop zone to a hidden observation point overlooking a likely area for Scud activity. When confirmed targets enter the area, SOC will be notified, and an E-2C Sentry's airborne warning and control system (AWACS) will vector strike aircraft into the target area. During their approach, the jets follow voice or signal beacon wavelengths to their prey. Air attacks will be conducted visually but any TELs obscured by darkness, camouflage, or poor weather will be lased, or "painted," by the recon team. Rolling in on their bomb runs, the fast–movers' sensors will lock on a laser guided bomb or rocket and release the "smart" munitions to glide along the laser's invisible path like a road map to the target. The jets will then maneuver away from the area, having only teased the outer perimeters of the lethal antiaircraft systems' kill zones, and the DELTA troopers, if necessary, will continue to lase targets for incoming aircraft from their concealed hideout. As many Iraqi units found out, the laser's invisible beam brought very visible destruction.

Reaching the austere departure airfield, the team is ushered into a secured hangar cordoned off from the rest of the facility. It is here that all of the specialized gear needed for the mission is stored. The departure airfield will also be the mission support site (MSS) for the operation, and a mobile communications van, mated to the main SOC communications bunker at King Khalid Military City,* has been moved into the hangar. The mobile van constitutes part of a duplex communications network

*Designed and constructed by the US Army Corps of Engineers during the Iran–Iraq War, King Khalid Military City is one of three huge base complexes around which the outer defenses of the kingdom are formed. The "Emerald City" (as it was called by many US soldiers, who were surprised at the sight of it rising out of the desert wastes) is located roughly 110 miles southwest of Kuwait's westernmost point almost halfway to the major Saudi Arabian city of Buraydah.

(**Above**) The control and reporting center outside King Khalid Military City which linked US and Saudi mobile and airborne communications. (**Left**) An internal view.

that ensured reception of the team's vital intelligence even if one part of the network went down from either systems failure or enemy action. Except for the team's communications specialist, who is coordinating preselected frequencies and transmission times, the troopers take little notice of the signals experts moving to and from the van and stay focused on checking and rechecking their weapons and field gear. All weapons had been test–fired before leaving the isolation site, and at the hangar, a ritual of sorts takes place, which will wed the jumper to his air items and other essential equipment. This union ends only when the mission is completed—or worse.

The six troopers wear sterile desert camouflage fatigues with the required face scarves and flop hats. Struggling mightily, they pull on cumbersome, insulated jumpsuits to help fight off the cold which sometimes exceeds –50 degrees at 35,000 feet, even in the Middle East. In addition to its insulation properties, the jumpsuits have radar–absorbing capabilities that will impede the enemy's ability to pick up the soldiers as they glide across the sky. Fortunately, the February night—cold even in the desert—engulfs the airfield, providing a small amount of relief as they don their main and reserve parachutes and oxygen masks. Before high–altitude drops like this one, both the jumpers and the crew of the unpressurized aircraft have to start breathing oxygen one hour before takeoff or "launch time." The team receives final jumpmaster inspections, and the troop commander arrives for that one last visit a leader makes. He is more of a fellow member than a commander, and everyone in the hangar knows the way the boss feels. He'd trade in his major's oak leaves to be going with them into Iraq.

Following the safety NCO out into the desert darkness, each man finds his own release to the inevitable tension. A flick of a "bird" finger to the top sergeant with a muffled, "Up yours, Top," or "See ya at the NCO club," mark the beginning of another mission. Their transportation, a huge C-141B, rests majestically next to the hangar, its gaping clamshell doors exposing the broad tail. The team struggles up the StarLifter's ramp into the cavernous cargo bay, while the crew chief and loadmaster guide the men around the small patches of hydraulic fluid habitually dotting its deck. An oxygen console rests securely in the center of the compartment, and each jumper

A C-141 prepares for a night takeoff from an airstrip in the Saudi desert.

plugs into it after disconnecting the oxygen mask from his individual bailout bottle.

As the StarLifter slowly pivots and then begins to taxi, the crew chief switches the internal lighting to the red lights required for the team to gain their night vision. The pilot reaches the main runway, and as he revs up the four powerful Pratt & Whitney turbofans for takeoff, each team member is caught in the thoughts of the moment: the myriad details that must be covered so that the mission succeeds, his wife, family, or the girl back home— the same thoughts soldiers have had to deal with since the second–oldest profession began.

The Jump

The C-141B flies on an easterly heading to its rendezvous point with two B-52s flying in from the tiny island base of Diego Garcia deep in the Indian Ocean. Snuggling into the number three slot, the formation portrays just another inbound bomber formation for any Iraqi radar still operating.

As the unlikely trio nears Iraqi airspace, the jumpmaster receives updates from the navigator. At prescribed checkpoints, he notifies the team of their exact coordinates so that all know where they are in the event that they are forced to bail out early. Thirty minutes from jump time, the team prepares for the "infil." The men assist each other in making sure that their rucksacks ride snugly against the bottom of the main parachute. Checking their padded-leather jump helmets, goggles, and oxygen masks one last time, they prepare to change over from the oxygen consoles to the bailout bottle strapped to their left sides. On command from the jumpmaster, the jumpers switch to their bailout bottles and waddle toward the open troop doors on each side of the fuselage.

Staff Sergeant Len Rodgers and the rest of the recon team work their way to positions along the walls of the StarLifter as their communications man, serving as jumpmaster, completes his visual checks and gives the hand signal for "Stand by." The cabin's eerie red lights, green jump light, and the howling winds whipping in the open troop doors could easily meet the needs of a good nightmare, and Staff Sergeant Rodgers is nearly deafened by the roaring wind and mournful banshee whine of the engines. He marvels that some people actually think this is fun! Moving closer to the door, he receives the "Go!" signal, as the jumpmaster disappears out the open troop door.

Pivoting on the ball of his right foot, Rodgers swings out behind him and falls into the position commonly referred to as the "frog." He's immediately followed in quick succession by the rest of the team. Plummeting through the moonless night, arms and legs extended, Rodgers begins to feel the penetrating cold. Behind him, each man monitors the altimeter securely strapped to his left wrist and assumes the glide position as they prepare to deploy their parachutes. At 30,000 feet, the aerial ballet continues as the team members pull their silver ripcords.

To the casual observer, this particular maneuver looks like a giant hand shaking each jumper loose from his very life. In reality, the men feel very little, and each checks the double-layer canopy above to see if his is fully inflated. Fortunately for this team, all now resemble airfoil-shaped wings, and the jumpers line up in a rough, follow-the-leader formation, taking the planned westerly heading as Staff Sergeant Rodgers navigates through the frozen night air. Settling into the parachute harness, he scans the panorama unfolding before him. Far to the north, flashes appear from the bombing mission the team's C-141 had joined. Craning his neck around to the southeast, he can barely make out green* tracers darting skyward in a futile search for the destroyers of a known Scud site's command and control bunker and wonders if it was done in by one of the F-117 stealth attack aircraft. He turns back and looks toward the unseen drop zone and toys with the idea that the display is for their benefit. He knows,

---

*Munitions manufactured by former Warsaw Pact countries such as the Soviet Union and Czechoslovakia give off green tracers, but the spectrum of hues sometimes runs to a yellow-green. US and many Western munitions give off a red trace.

however, that the distant explosions mean that real, flesh–and–blood men are dying.

As the team continues on its noiseless flight, each jumper lines up on the dull luminescent strip on the helmet below. Altimeter checks show that the gradual warming they feel is due to the descent. At 12,000 feet, they remove their individual masks and inhale the night air. With each passing minute, the team gets closer to the drop zone. This is when the paratroopers are most vulnerable. All are sure that the entire Iraqi Army is waiting to pounce on them, but the only living things awaiting the DELTA troopers are some stray goats from a Bedouin camp that run bleating into the night when they strike the earth. The men are relieved

Special Forces trooper on a practice jump, taking up the "frog" position. Note that the soldier wears an altimeter on his left wrist. Rucksacks are always strapped below the main parachutes and, in the second photo, a rucksack can be seen dangling fifteen feet below the jumper so that it will be out of his way when he lands.

that no reception committee is on hand to greet them, but there will be plenty of time for surprises. One of the greatest shocks of this desert war for the special operations soldiers was the fact that whenever you thought you were in the middle of nowhere, someone was always showing up—usually at the most inopportune time.

Chapter 6

The Scud Busters

The Lord said to Moses, "Send men to spy out the land of Canaan, . . . from each tribe of their fathers shall you send a man, everyone a leader among them."

Numbers 13

The team quickly assembles after landing. The troopers move to a nearby depression, and while half take up defensive positions, the others strip off their heavy jump suits and then roll them up with their 'chutes and jump helmets to make compact, easily buried bundles. The gear is quickly buried and the now–unencumbered troopers silently take their turn guarding the perimeter. Preparing to move out, each man goes through his mental checklist to ensure that every piece of equipment is in place. Faint vehicle noise drifts through the black night and the telltale signs of light are seen to the south.

Staff Sergeant Christopher Gleason, the point man for this operation, silently moves to his right, where the team leader is making last–minute com-

---

Troopers in the desert viewed through an image–intensification device.

---

pass checks and using his handheld satellite navigation system to pinpoint the team's exact location. Chief Warrant Officer Gary Van Hee intently studies the tiny screen's luminous, digital readout, which arrived as coded signals from a Global Positioning System (GPS) satellite drifting in orbit above the desert. Only one–third of the complete twenty–four–satelite constellation needed to blanket the earth had yet been sent aloft, so the lack of full–time, three–dimensional coverage sometimes made reception problematic. Tonight, though, Van Hee is having no trouble and he smiles broadly as the staff sergeant moves within whisper distance.

Gleason points out the rather obvious activity to the southwest, "The whole place is crawling with ragheads, Chief!" Van Hee's camouflaged face breaks into a devious grin and he retorts with his typical, "No shit, Sherlock." The team leader's time–honored response reassures the edgy point man, who steps gingerly back to his position and prepares to move out.

Each man's personal equipment is designed for specific tasks. Black balaclavas have been replaced with desert flop hats and face paint of pale yellow and brown. "No sweat" bandanas and camouflage scarves are wrapped tightly around necks and tucked into the now–familiar "chocolate chip"–patterned camouflage jackets. The men carry ammunition in pouches hung from their vests, and distributed about their bodies are canteens, first–aid equipment, a powerful miniature flashlight, and a Beretta pistol. Two of the six–man team also carry silencers so that their Barettas can be used to noiselessly kill an enemy guard or nosey point man. The unique silencers are so efficient that, using subsonic rounds, only the sound of the hammer striking the firing pin and the gun's action cycling can be heard—a small sound in this noisy environment.

The threat of "getting slimed" by Iraqi poison gas is far more than rhetorical in this war, so each trooper also carries a gas mask, securely strapped within easy reach on his left leg, and a complete protective suit in his rucksack. Rucks for this mission are configured with extra ammunition and smoke grenades. Additional water, medical supplies, a small quantity of food, and limited decontamination gear, complete the major items. Personal weapons are based on the defensive requirements of the mission, and the team carries either Colt M16A2 assault rifles or Heckler & Koch MP5 submachine guns.

While these final checks are being made, the communications expert, Sergeant First Class Michael Cranson, sends the team's initial entry report, a codeword transmission advising the MSS that they have arrived safely at the drop zone. For this signal, Cranson uses his radio's burst–transmission capability, and with the touch of a finger, the pre-coded message is instantaneously sent. The split–second broadcast provides no time for hostile direction finders to get a fix on the team's position.

Armed with an integrally silenced MP5 SD3, Staff Sergeant Gleason slowly leads the way out of the depression and toward a large, rocky outcropping. The team members swing into their allotted positions behind him, forming a loose file. This and every action these soldiers will complete during the mission has been practiced over and over. Gleason and his fellow troopers use AN/PVS-7 night vision goggles to guide them through the rocky terrain. Popularly known as NODs, for night observation devices, the 1.5 pound goggles fit against a trooper's forehead and literally turn the desert darkness into a greenish, but very visible, day.

A Global Positioning System receiver.

By amplifying existing light, they enable man–sized targets to be recognized at almost 100 yards on all but the very darkest nights, with good moonlight extending their range by fifty percent or more. Operating under a last quarter moon, the men can see extremely well, but spotty cloud cover creates sudden, unexpected drops in visibility, in addition to the device's limited peripheral field of vision.

The point man's stubby, silenced MP5, his night vision goggles, and modified tactical vest give him an unearthly appearance. The bleak terrain, coupled with the patrol's appearance, could easily be mistaken for a Hollywood supernatural thriller. Walking behind the point man, the compass man, Staff Sergeant Rodgers, not only navigates for the patrol with his compass (for direction) and altimeter (for elevation), but also by watching his distance count (by how far he walks). The team leader occupies the number three position, and his communications, or "commo" man, Sergeant First Class Cranson, holds down number four. Positions five and six are rounded out by the team medic, Master Sergeant Frank Rodrigues, and the demolitions expert, another staff sergeant, who doubles as the patrol's tail gunner. His primary responsibility is to ensure that no one surprises the team from the rear and, like the point man, the tail gunner also resembles an alien stalking through a moonscape.

While approaching the low ridge where they will set up their observation post, it becomes painfully clear that they have, indeed, dropped into an area full of Iraqi units. Reaching their destination, the team immediately sets up security, sends out a two–man recon of the area, and digs in (one of the veterans later likened the experience to hacking into an asphalt parking lot). Flexible prefabricated covers are stretched over their holes to make the hide site complete, and the men will use disposable plastic bags to contain their bodily wastes so that no wild or stray animals will be attracted to their position— a potentially disasterous occurrence that could attract curious Iraqi eyes and expose their position.

The troopers are prepared to lie low for days, watching for the elusive Scuds, but the arrival of dawn quickly reveals that part of Saddam's missile inventory is already operating in this area.

At first, only normal military, and civilian, traffic can be seen speeding along the east–west highway stretched out before them. It isn't long, though, before Van Hee recognizes some very familiar friends. Tailing along behind a westbound string of large civilian Mercedes tractor–trailers is a Ural-375 truck, mounting a mobile crane, and a pair of Type ZIL-157V tractors hauling elongated cargoes covered by tarps. The vehicles continue down the road for almost two miles and then pull off to the right about a hundred yards into the desert. Excitement is running high in the team and reaches a peak a half hour later when an eight–wheeled MAZ-543 transporter–erector–launcher (a TEL vehicle known to carry Scud missiles) and a ZIL-157V tanker towing a trailer appear to the east. They zoom by and continue on to the other waiting vehicles which, by now, include numerous supply trucks, C^3 vans, and a mix of towed quad 23mm and dual 30mm antiaircraft guns in the process of deploying on both sides of the highway. The top of the TEL is still well–covered by sand–colored tarps, but Van Hee is willing to bet his life and the lives of his men that it mounts a Scud missile.

The suspicious TEL remains with the other vehicles for only about ten minutes before all but the antiaircraft element suddenly begin to move off in column across the desert. After only a few hundred yards, the lead truck turns abruptly to the left into a deep wadi that arches back toward the road passing under it at a long, thin bridge a quarter mile past their original turnoff. As far as the team leader's concerned, this confirms it. There is no reason for an Iraqi unit this far afield of the main weight of coalition air attacks to go to this kind of trouble to hide itself unless it's a missile unit. At night, the TEL and select support vehicles will emerge back onto the flat, tabletop terrain to fire its terror weapon at Israel.

Sighting through his 7x40 Steiner binoculars, Van Hee begins to list what he sees as the vehicles disappear one by one down the now–apparent path bulldozed to the dry streambed. His time as an exchange member with one of West Germany's famed long–range reconnaissance companies is now paying off. As he reels off the NATO names, the team's radio operator writes them on his notepad. After one more sweep of the target area, Van Hee tells Cranson to inform headquarters that the "mother of all targets" is in front of them. He then slides back into the two–man foxhole, closes his eyes, and wearily tries to relax.

Opening his rucksack flap, Cranson closely examines the Satellite Communications System (SATCOM). From the ruck's outside pocket he pulls a miniature black satellite antenna folded in such a way that it looks like little more than a small, closed umbrella. Unfolding its legs and arms, Cranson places the device just beyond the lip of the hide hole and checks its frame to ensure that each prong is extended to its maximum position. With a diameter of only 17in, the antenna's profile will provide an observer with little clue as to what it is, even if the device could be seen from the highway. Cranson plugs the antenna's black, coaxial cable into the SATCOM and turns it on.

While the system hums and ticks through its self–checks and calibrations, the commo man listens through his headsets and consults the *Equatorial Satelite Antenna Pointing Guide* for the necessary elevation and azimuth angles required to orient the SATCOM's antenna for sending and receiving signals. Cranson moves the frame dish back and forth until he hears the unmistakable peep of the orbiting satel-

lite and then settles in to start his transmission. He speaks in slow, distinct tones into his microphone, sending the entire intelligence picture of what the recon team is viewing to a receiving station in the SOC communications bunker at King Khalid. Immediately, this vital information is passed through the US Air Force liaison officer to CENTCOM's air component tucked away in a basement corner of the Royal Saudi Air Force building in Riyadh.

Within minutes of the initial report being sent, coalition jets, pulled from the air campaign to hunt for Scuds, are vectored from their stations as others scramble from Saudi fields far to the southeast. Twenty–two minutes after the initial report, the first aircraft arrive over the highway. The jets briefly circle well out of range of the frustrated Iraqi anti-aircraft gunners while coordinating their attack, and then make straight for the well–camouflaged vehicles parked along the dry streambed.

Tipped off to the Iraqis' exact location, the ungainly looking A-10 Thunderbolt IIs (affectionately

A man–portable satelite communications system.

Mission accomplished. (**Left**) A missile and its mobile launching platform caught out in the open and destroyed. (**Above**) A missile rearm vehicle burned to the ground by Air Force jets.

called "Warthogs" or simply "Hogs") turn the wadi into a death trap. Resembling sharks during a feeding frenzy, the jets continuously roll in and pound the missile unit, and then begin to work on targets of opportunity up and down the highway. Their method of attack, however, seems strange to the hidden team members watching the show with intense interest. All had at one time or another seen live–fire exercises where the hog drivers swooped in and plastered targets from treetop heights, but now their hogs seemed to rarely venture below 8,000 or 10,000 feet because of the antiair assets.

Throughout the rest of the day, air strikes continue to hit what can only be described as "a target–rich environment." Periodic, huge explosions rend the wadi, and Cranson, who is monitoring the Warthogs' communications net, informs Van Hee that the hog drivers claim "two Scuds TANGO UNIFORM" (Tits Up—slang for "destroyed"). Later strikes are conducted almost exclusively by F-16s, with some help from Tornado attack aircraft of unknown origin. The team hadn't been briefed that

Tornadoes would be in on the show, and although Cranson picks up their cryptic transmissions, he can only state that they are *not* speaking *American* English. He can't make out if they are piloted by Brits, Saudis, or Italians (all of whom field the multirole jet), and is the butt of several rude jokes from his friends until they, too, fail just as badly at deciphering the jet jockeys' nationalities.

These aircraft, and all others working the many targets, fly no lower than the Warthogs and, consequently, there are a lot of misses. But even through the smoke and dust kicked up by the strikes, Van Hee can clearly see that the cumulative weight of the air attacks has destroyed nearly every vehicle in the area by using a combination of rockets, iron bombs, and cluster munitions. The medium–altitude attacks have, moreover, rendered the defenders' antiaircraft guns nearly useless by striking from beyond their *effective* range. No one in the team sees any coalition aircraft go down.

As evening draws near, the team leader fears that their position is becoming increasingly vulnerable.

(**Opposite**) A night–stalking F-15 taking on fuel during *Desert Storm*. (**Above**) A disabled fuel truck in Iraq, and (**left**) an actual Scud TEL targeted by an F-15E. Target identification was often extremely difficult at night, even with the most sophisticated ground and airborne systems.

Although well–hidden on a barely perceptible ridge, they are, nevertheless, located on the highest terrain feature in the area. It might only be a matter of time before the increasingly active Iraqi patrols unearth them. As soon as it begins to turn dark, the team picks up their gear, quickly sanitizes the area, and heads south across the previously active road, now silent except for the crackling of a few vehicle fires still burning brightly. Moving carefully across undulating ground, the team settles into a steady, cautious march. Upon reaching a small depression dotted with low, thorny bushes, they form a perimeter and rest before continuing on to the exfiltration point that night.

But this is as far as they get. Gleason detects the hot thermal images of several trucks pulling off the highway barely 1,500 yards directly behind them. Both Gleason and Van Hee carry handheld AN/PAS-7 thermal viewers that pick up the heat of the vehicles several hundred yards beyond the system's stated range (the trucks can't be seen at all by the shorter–range NODs except for the occasional glint of reflected moonlight). Almost immediately, they are joined by a larger, semitrailer–sized vehicle.

Could it be another Scud TEL? Through their two thermal viewers, the team watches with nervous excitement—and no small amount of glee—as what appears to be more Scud launchers and support vehicles trickle in. Although the glowing, red, negative images provided by the viewers cannot produce an accurate picture at that distance, Van Hee and crew believe that their new neighbor is a full-blown battery preparing to launch a nasty surprise at the Jewish State.

Under normal circumstances, the lack of clear, sharp images would not prevent the team from determining if this is a Scud battery. With even the little elevation provided by a slight rise, they could look down on the spread of vehicles and make out the telltale signs unique to that type of unit's deployment pattern. Unfortunately, the recon team not only lacks altitude now, but is, in fact, slightly lower than the Iraqis. From their essentially eye-level view, all they can tell is that there are several dozen vehicles—some quite large—arrayed to the north.

Whoever they are, the darkness of night has given them a false sense of security and Van Hee can make out that they are neither properly dispersed nor making any effort at concealment. The team can easily call an air strike in on this unit, but even though the Iraqis are currently not well-dispersed, that could change in an instant. Moreover, if this is a Scud battery, even the fast-movers viewing the target area through their Maverick missiles' powerful infrared sensors will have great difficulty picking out the critical launch vehicles which, it turns out, are almost indistinguishable from fuel trucks and other lengthy vehicles at attack distances. Blanketing the area with cluster bombs will not guarantee the destruction of the mobile launchers either, although it would certainly "attrit" their crews and support personnel.

For obvious reasons, the Air Force was having a terrible time tracking down the nocturnal TELs and, true to the black humor that befriends men in war, the troopers nearly busted a gut a week earlier when they learned that a group of Jordanian tractor-trailer rigs had been rocketed and cluster-bombed when mistaken for one of Saddam's Scud units. It seems that their hapless drivers had pulled off the highway at one of its infrequent rest stops late at night and were inadvertently mistaken for a rearm and refuel site.* A Special Forces team on the ground soon confirmed that the blasted vehicles were civilian and, in any event, the Iraqis had immediately bussed foreign journalists to the scene to record "President Bush's most vile outrage." Word spread quickly from King Khalid "Emerald City" to the intelligence analysts, working out of prefab buildings on a Riyadh soccer field, and the shocked air unit that made the strike.

---

*If there was a plus side to the mistaken attack, it was the fact that fewer civilian drivers were now willing to brave the highway at night, thus making the job of target identification slightly less complicated.

Now, Van Hee finds the tables completely turned. Although the team leader is considerably closer than any fighter jockey releasing a Maverick missile and has all the time in the world to examine the glowing, shapes, there is no way he can confirm that they are what he believes them to be. Van Hee needs to know exactly what he is looking at before he calls in the fast–movers. Once committed to a strike here, on what is perhaps just some inconsequential heavy–lift unit, there might not be enough time or available air assets to immediately respond if a genuine Scud battery is detected.

Van Hee instructs Rodrigues and the tail gunner to move back toward the highway, to get a closer look, and hands over his thermal viewer. He wishes his team had gotten another of the precious thermal systems but is thankful that they

were able to get any at all. Many Special Forces long–range reconnaissance patrols didn't even have one of the scarce AN/PAS-7s, but the highly critical nature of DELTA's scud–hunting mission allowed Van Hee to get his mitts on two of the lightweight devices.

Gleason watches as their ghostly figures silently disappear into another depression, and settles into what is likely to be a long vigil on the perimeter. Everyone understands that the men may have to move in as close as 200 or 250 yards before their viewer will let them confirm the team's suspicions. If the approach to the Iraqi unit is difficult, the men might be gone for many hours. During their absence, the team checks and rehecks its equipment and notifies SOC of the situation.

The waiting is mercifully short. Helpful terrain features and a surprising lack of security have allowed the scouts to get their job done in barely three hours. Rodrigues reports that at least two of the mystery vehicles are "Spud" TELs, and Van Hee wastes no time setting back out with him to a spot where Rodrigues is confident that each of the confirmed launchers can be painted for incoming aircraft. When Gleason first spotted the gathering Iraqi vehicles at roughly 1,500 yards, they were beyond the effective range of Van Hee's AN/PAQ-3 MULE target designator, and the laser team has to travel almost one–third of the way back toward the road to ensure that their instrument can get a clear fix on the TELs. Newer, experimental handheld designators, that can accurately illuminate targets at roughly three times the distance had recently been sent to the Gulf, but Van Hee's team are not among the lucky few to receive one.

The route back is well known by this time, and the men are able to move with deliberate haste. The midnight hour Iraq often uses for launching its terror weapons is fast approaching, and through

A Scud missile erect on its launcher and ready to fire.

AN/AVS-6 Aviator's
night–vision imaging system

Comparative imagery from night vision equipment used by US forces in *Desert Storm*: (**top**) unaided, daylight photograph of an M606 Jeep and the same vehicle shot from a slightly different angle through (**center**) image intensification and (**bottom**) infrared devices.

AN/PVS-7A
Night vision goggles

AN/PAQ-3 Modular universal laser
equipment (MULE) target designator

AN/PAS-7 Thermal viewer

their thermal viewers, both the laser team and Gleason, at the hastily established patrol base, can see the unmistakable pillar of a missile raised on one of the erectors. A brief break in the clouds also allows a faint, grainy image to be seen from the NODs.

At the base, Rodgers peers intently at the shadowy image of assembled Iraqi vehicles and nervously fingers his M16. From his vantage point, he can see only one other trooper, the tail gunner, about twenty yards to his right, who has turned his way, as well, and gives Rodgers a thumbs up. Rodgers knows that he isn't the only man wondering if the fast–movers will make it before the Iraqis launch. He doesn't feel

himself to be particularly expendable and hopes that the Air Force will refrain from using cluster munitions against close–in, ground–lased targets as the team had been briefed before the mission.

Activity suddenly picks up near the road. Several of the smaller Iraqi vehicles start hauling off in all directions and a lone, dual 30mm antiaircraft gun, positioned slightly east of the launch site, begins to pop green tracers into the air. The team watches, mesmerized from their ringside seats as other antiaircraft artillery, or "triple–A," quickly comes to life, sending aloft crisscrossing streams of fire. Cranson, meanwhile, listens in on the approaching jets transmission: "Honey 1, sixty seconds, Maverick. . . . Honey 1, ten seconds. . . . Honey 1, laser on. . . . Spot. . . . Honey 1, lock–launch." *

The men have almost grown accustomed to the awe–inspiring spectacle of light and sound when a huge, double explosion bursts skyward. A Maverick air–to–ground missile has slammed into a TEL and ignited its fueled–up weapon.

Most of the triple–A falls silent for what seems like a long time, but one Iraqi gunner recovers from the shock of the explosion almost immediately and resumes shooting even before the fireball disappears into the air. Long strings of triple–A again arch into the sky as Rodgers and the others watch in fascination, knowing that Van Hee is already painting another Scud: "Honey 2, spot. . . . Lock–launch. . . . Honey 2, terminate." ** A second huge explosion lights the scene and more vehicles can be seen scurrying away from the carnage. As far as the Iraqi grunts are concerned, all Saddam's "little toys" do is attract death from above.

Secondary explosions begin to rock the target area as the laser team moves at a steady trot toward the patrol base. The Air Force is holding back from dropping its deadly packages of cluster bombs, to give them a jump at getting away from the target. Rodrigues and Van Hee's glowing green images can be seen quite clearly during their last 100–meter dash to the base, and some of the troopers can't refrain from greeting them with low–volume (*very* low–volume) whoops and hollers as they clear the perimeter. As if to join in the congratulations, the Air Force begins to hit the site again, and now the whole team moves out at a run. The troopers haven't covered a quarter mile when suddenly,

while cresting a wide ripple in the earth, they smack into an Iraqi squad barely thirty yards away. The Iraqis were apparently on patrol when the air strike erupted and are riding out the fireworks in this shallow depression.

The startled team comes under fire. Dropping to one knee, Gleason pumps two 9mm rounds into the nearest Iraqi's chest. Without pausing, he switches to the next target, who immediately crumples into a heap, his stomach perforated by two slugs from Gleason's H&K. Immediately sizing up the situation, Van Hee yells for the team to break contact. While moving through their leapfrog maneuver, a lucky round from an RPG-7 shoulder–fired rocket launcher lands between Rodgers and the tail gunner. Although most of the explosion is absorbed by the ground, shrapnel rips into Rodgers' right side and the tail gunner is killed instantly by a dime–sized piece of metal piercing his skull just above the right eye.

The four unhurt troopers immediately lay down an intense base of fire, which convinces the Iraqis to fall back to less dangerous surroundings. The firefight has lasted less than two minutes. One American is dead and another's life is leaking into the rocky earth. Hauling Rodgers and the fallen trooper along with them, the team hurriedly resumes their escape south while Air Force jets strike at Iraqi vehicles streaking pell–mell through the area. It is painfully obvious to all that they are in deep trouble, and, if action is not taken quickly, will either be killed or wind up being displayed on the evening news as prisoners of war.

Air–ground communications between the team and SOC is now being maintained by a "fast FAC," or forward air controller, who passes word to Cranson that immediate efforts are being initiated to get them out. They are instructed to keep moving south without delay, but each man knows that they are faced with a decision no soldier wants to make.

---

* "Sixty seconds to laser designator switch–on. . . . Ten seconds to switch–on. . . . Laser spot acquired. . . . Target locked–on and ordnance fired."

** "Laser spot acquired. . . . Target locked–on and ordnance fired. . . . Have visual contact; laser no longer needed."

The venerable A-10 Thunderbolt II "Warthog" and DELTA formed a deadly Scud hunter–killer team in Iraq. A-10s also proved themselves to be an effective search and rescue asset.

The young trooper's body hinders their movement to the extraction point, and they decide to bury him as quickly as possible. In a lonely defile, the team digs a grave for their comrade. It is not very much, as graves go, but it is made with love and respect, and the men dig as deeply as time will permit. Wrapping the staff sergeant up in his poncho liner, they gently lay his body into the desert soil. Van Hee carefully checks, then rechecks, the tight ten–digit grid coordinate he has plotted for the unmarked grave and silently swears to his fallen trooper that he'll be back for him. The team says a quick prayer over their friend, and then, carrying Rodgers, they strike out south again. Rodrigues, the team's medic, recognizes that the multiple shrapnel wounds are worse than previously thought. Rodgers is slipping in and out of consciousness and losing blood. Cranson radios the fast FAC that they have a man who will die if they don't get him out soon.

SOC knows that no special operations helicopters are currently available for a quick recovery, nor are there likely to be any until almost mid–morning. Virtually everything is already committed to the far–flung operations in progress throughout what the Israelis call "Scudinavia" in western Iraq. SOC decides to use a MC-130 Combat Talon equipped with a Fulton Recovery System to conduct a surface–to–air recovery (STAR) of Rodgers. This is not generally a preferred method of extraction because it takes so much time to set up the Fulton and is easily seen, but with helo assets unavailable, Rodgers' condition makes it necessary. Alerting the 1st Special Operations Wing, a hasty plan is worked out to recover the wounded DELTA trooper.

The Extractions

Arar Royal Military Airfield near Banadah is the launch site of some of *Desert Storm's* most inventive operations. It's not an unusual place to find one or two of the 1st Special Operations Wing's MC-130s, and when the call comes down, immediate preparations are made for the STAR. First, a modified delivery canister resembling an old napalm bomb is loaded with all the items needed by the team to set

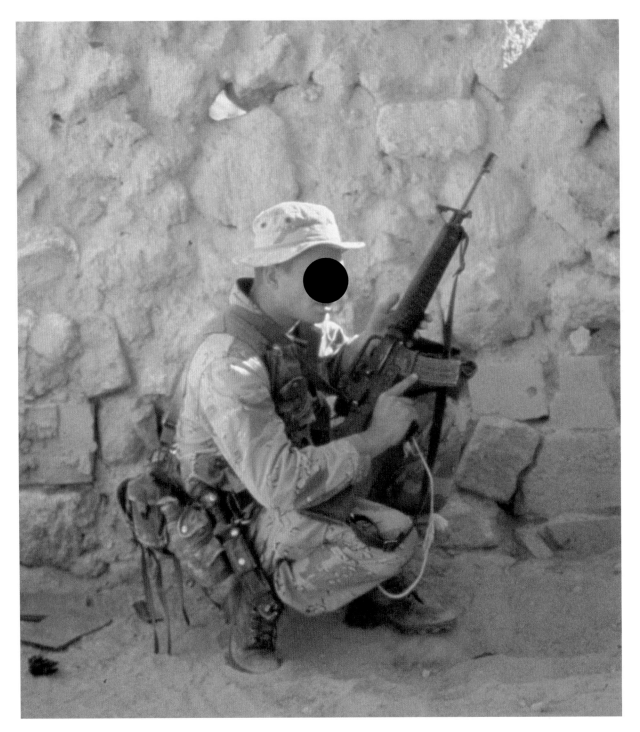

(**Opposite**) Intense concentration marks the face of a trooper keeping watch on the surrounding terrain from a desert ruin. (**Right**) An E-3A Sentry at Dhahran, Saudi Arabia.

up the recovery. The canister is then affixed to a waiting A-10's weapons pylon, and the Warthog is immediately launched toward western Iraq. As the "Sandy"* Hog driver and his wingman speed north, the crew of the MC-130 receives their mission brief. Not uncharacteristically, the crew takes the briefing quite professionally; yet, underneath their calm exterior, there is a surge of adrenalin. They are going to execute a mission that they have trained hard for and has not been performed in combat for nearly twenty years. The airmen are confident that the improvements in technique and hardware introduced since the Vietnam War are sound.

Already deep in the desert, the recon team is now told to move beyond their original pickup point into an even more desolate area well away from any known military targets. After several hours, the exhausted team comes upon a group of ruined dwellings and sets up defensive positions as dawn begins to break. Rodrigues has just changed Rodgers' I-V and is connecting a new bag of saline solution when Cranson's radio crackles to life. The Sandy pilot is attempting to contact the team. Hopefully, it will appear to any nearby Iraqis that the hog driver and his wingman are out hunting for targets of opportunity and will avoid any curious overtures.

Van Hee is informed that he should mark their position for a "delivery." Using a mirror, Van Hee

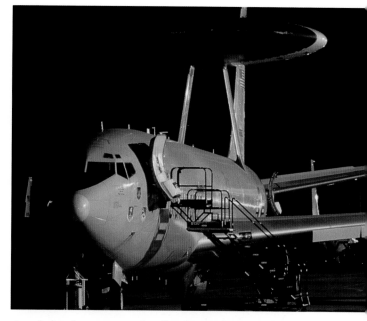

signals his location to the Sandys performing their lazy search pattern well away from the team. After receiving an acknowledgment from the pilot, Van Hee moves out about 175 yards from the perimeter, places a single orange panel in the gravel, and immediately moves back to the shelter of the ruins. The pair of Warthogs are continuing their indirect meander toward the ruins when they spot a group of Iraqi trucks moving parallel to the team approximately two miles out. Although they do not appear to be looking for the troopers, the Sandys take no chances and proceed to spoil the Iraqis' morning with fire from their 30mm Gatling nose cannons. As the hogs leave the burning vehicles, they approach the ruins indirectly by flying in a low, wide arc that, hopefully, will not draw attention to the hidden Americans. No extra passes are made over the site and the equipment canister is "pickled off" as the ugly jets roar overhead.

Thirty minutes behind the Sandys, the MC-130 Combat Talon penetrates into "Injun Country." While passing over the berm line, the special opera-

---

*An A-10 pilot specially trained for rescue escort (RESCORT) missions. The rugged A-10's ability to loiter for extended periods of time makes it a perfect aircraft for conducting searches in a high-threat environment, and Sandy's are experts at locating survivors. By marking target locations and supressing enemy fire, they allow more vulnerable rescue aircraft to do their job. The term originated during the Vietnam war as a call sign used by A-1E Skyraider pilots providing gunfire suppression during rescue operations.

A surface–to–air recovery (STAR) of two troopers using a Fulton extraction system: (**Top row**) A canister containing the system is dropped by an Air Force fast–mover.' Helium bottles, balloon, line and attached suit in a recovered canister. The guard cables and whisker–like probes of an MC-130 yoke, opened to snare the Fulton's line. (**Center row**) Two volunteers with "Are we really going to do this?" looks on their faces. The line being snagged. Up, up, and away! (**Left**) The open rear ramp of the receiving aircraft as the soldiers are hauled aboard.

tions aircraft receives an ominous radio report from the E-3A Sentry orbiting in Saudi airspace behind them. Electronic warfare officers operating the AWACS's highly sophisticated sensors detect a number of hostile radar impulses. Despite the fact that the Air Force owns the sky, being painted over Iraqi territory always causes concern. Most of the Talon's crew had friends on the ill–fated AC-130 Specter gunship that failed to get out of Kuwaiti airspace when "locked on" by a surface–to–air missile. The result was charred debris floating in the Gulf and no survivors.

As the Talon closes on the team's location, Van Hee and Gleason open the canister. Extracting its contents, they find a balloon, nylon line, harness, and suit along with a bottle of helium. Rodrigues checks Rodgers' condition while Van Hee and Gleason prepare to inflate the balloon, and Cranson makes contact with the inbound Talon. Not only is the MC-130 approaching, but the pair of A-10s continue to ply the area in ostensibly random patterns, and a flight of F-16s has already assumed a guardian–angel role well to the east but within easy striking distance if trouble develops. The Warthogs again cruise past the ruins while Van Hee and Gleason affix the helium bottle to the balloon that will stretch Rodgers' lifeline in reach of the specially equipped rescue aircraft. As it inflates, the bulbous cream and silver balloon takes on the shape of a giant fish, its floppy fins growing firmer with each passing second.

While all this is going on, Rodrigues and Cranson gingerly ease Rodgers into the olive green recovery suit sewn firmly to the Fulton's harness. As its furlined hood is placed around Rodger's face, his glazed eyes open slightly to Rodrigues' familiar grin and thick, angular eyebrows. His medic friend has been in DELTA for a long time and has a well-earned reputation as a battlefield doctor. Patting Rodgers' thigh, he says with a chuckle, "You gonna go on a neat ride, my man. It's up, up, and away for you." Rodrigues does his best to put up a brave front for his buddy but fears that Rodgers may have lost too much blood. The furlined face is gray and expressionless, but it seems for a moment that he tries to acknowledge what the medic is saying.

Twenty minutes from the pickup, the balloon is allowed to creep slowly skyward. It reaches its full height and Rodgers sits securely attached to its tether while the team, minus the doc, stands guard in a circle resembling a herd of buffaloes shielding a wounded calf. Rodrigues continues his lively chatter to help keep his patient awake and gently pats and strokes his unhurt left arm. Although he doesn't know it, his determined "woofing" is paying off. Rodgers dimly comprehends that his buddies are doing everything they can for him and takes some comfort from the New Yorker's verbal blizzard.

At 525 feet in the air, the balloon attached to the tethered nylon rope is a beacon for all to see and is the reason that the team had to put so much distance between themselves and the highway. The incoming MC-130's unusual nose now resembles a snout with two large whiskers. These whiskers are actually probes swung outward to form the yoke. Their main function is to guide the line into place at the center of the nose as the plane makes the pickup.

Cautiously lining up on the balloon, the pilot throttles the fat, four-engine airplane down to 112, 105, then only 97 knots for the pickup and aims at the target area on the nylon rope marked by three orange streamers. Striking the target markers, the probes guide the line to the yoke and secure it as the plane flies over the DELTA team. With a minimum of fanfare, Rodgers is literally snatched from the gravity of earth and appears as a small dot hurtling behind the Talon. While the STAR is a nerve-wracking affair for the soldiers to watch, they know that Rodgers actually experiences less of a jolt during the pickup than he did when he opened his parachute.

In the gaping cargo bay, the loadmaster and crew chief now prepare to winch their human cargo on board. The nylon line is pressed firmly against the Talon's belly by the rush of air, and inside the bay, the crew chief and loadmaster move quickly to hook it, much as one snaps a fishing line. Reeling

A special operations helicopter streaking at low level across the night sky.

in the line and attaching it to the Talon's internal, hydraulic winch, the precious cargo is slowly drawn into the cargo bay. Soon, Rodgers is lying in the safety of the aircraft while Air Force Reserve trauma specialists work frantically to stabilize him. The only hitch during the pickup occurs when the balloon fails to release from the line. The Talon's navigator is forced to spear the playfully bouncing object with a harpoon–like device and cut it free with the help of the loadmaster.

As the MC-130 speeds toward friendly airspace, the remainder of the recon team moves out.

A well–timed air operation, centered mainly along the highway to the north, is initiated by the F-16s and a fresh pair of A-10s to mask their movement and the troopers head south by southwest toward a new pickup point several miles away. Although appropriate helo assets will be available in a few hours, SOC has decided to not make the extraction until after dark since Rodgers has been rescued and the recon team is in no immediate danger.

The team had flung their prefabricated hide site covers into their foxholes and buried them when they sanitized their original position, but the rough terrain the men are now moving into offers many opportunities for natural concealment and there is no worry that they no longer have the prefabs. They soon come upon a wadi that offers a reasonable amount of security and decide that it is as good a place as any to go to ground till nightfall. After the midnight firefight, Saddam's forces know that American commandos are in the area, but ongoing airstrikes have given the Iraqis plenty of other things to worry about, and their movement has been heavily restricted for scores of miles in all directions.

The only enemy assaulting the men is a determined legion of sandfleas, which tirelessly press their attack as "big red" moved slowly across the sky. They do, however, also receive periodic visits from various Air Force jets. The pilots make it a point to fly close enough to the DELTA team to scout for hostile forces, yet their seemingly random passes are conducted at varied–enough intervals to give no clue to the whereabouts of the hidden soldiers.

Night comes quickly in this part of the world and the already–cool late January temperature drops like a stone even before the sun disappears from the horizon. As the four men make their final equipment checks before moving out, help is crossing the Saudi–Iraqi border 100 miles to the southeast. Boring through the gathering fog at sixty feet off the ground, a lone MH-60 Black Hawk is finally on its way to retrieve the soldiers.

Almost ten hours has passed since Rodgers was extracted, and Van Hee's team starts to move south again. The welcome night engulfs the dirty, unshaven troopers and their night vision goggles allow them to move with the assurance of prowling nocturnal beasts unencumbered by darkness.

In spite of the sophisticated vision devices and their apparent isolation, the desert holds one more surprise. As they near the pickup point, a young goat herder casually emerges from a depression forty yards to their right. Upon seeing the ghost–like apparitions, he runs screaming through the darkness, scattering livestock in all directions. Fearing a return of Iraqi soldiers, the team moves through the area quickly and sets up a defensive perimeter 600 yards from their encounter. Speaking in hushed tones with the inbound chopper, Van Hee guides the bird in until the troopers can be seen on its infrared imager.

As the Black Hawk's wheels touch the hard–packed dirt, the remaining four troopers scramble aboard and slide across the metal floor plates to hold each other in the embrace only those who have faced the ultimate challenge know. "We made it!" Gleason yells above the pitch of the engines as the helicopter begins to rise above the desert floor.

After looking out of the waist gunner's hatch for any signs of Iraqi forces, Van Hee wearily leans back and says "Christ, I hope so."

Epilogue

Fort Bragg, North Carolina

Along Ardennes Road, framed by a stand of regal North Carolina pines, the John F. Kennedy Special Warfare Center Chapel occupies a place of dignity and serenity. Against the hustle and organized chaos that characterizes this sprawling Airborne post, it provides a safe haven of sanity and peace whether the visitor is a regular church–goer or just passing through.

Framed against the buildup of an incoming spring rain, a memorial service is taking place. It is a closed service designed to avoid the prying eyes of nosy newspaper reporters still trying to write a story connected to *Desert Storm*. Although the service was unannounced, the chapel is crowded. Word has passed quickly around the special operations community that one of their own is being remembered today. Conspicuous in their off–the–rack suits, cowboy boots, and nonregulation mustaches and haircuts, the members of a DELTA troop have gathered once more. Along with their wives, they are here to help the young widow weather one more storm. It is a unique scene—one that rarely occurred in the past few years but has often been repeated since the operations "over there."

The widow's five–year–old son, sandy blond hair neatly combed and out of character, sits on the edge of his front–row seat. Gently poking an imagined spot on the chapel's maroon carpet with the toe of his Sunday best, he absently wonders, not quite knowing or understanding why he is here. He is aware that his mom's world is in disarray, and her sadness is something he has never seen before. All he knows is that the man whose picture occupies the table in front of the chapel room is not coming home. His father left home late one night "on business." That was not an unusual occurrence in his young life, but now a new twist has occurred. Mom said that his best friend has gone to live with God forever.

A soldier is laid to rest.

His father's friends, gathered around the family in a supportive ring, knew the story all too well. The smiling young soldier, pictured with the coveted green beret had been their friend, and in this close-knit group of professionals, that one word, "friend," was all that required their loyalty.

The emotion of these men was not a complicated show. Each behaved simply but with a degree of maturity in combat that comes only to a veteran. They accepted what was thrown their way in a businesslike manner, hiding their hatred, fear, confusion, and pride behind the mantle of a well-trained special operations soldier. To this group and the many others like them, the specter of death was always an additional member of the team. In this particular case, their friend was no longer able to avoid death's embrace. Thousands of miles away, hidden in an unmarked grave deep in Iraq's rugged western province, their trusted friend and the young boy's father had rested until a subsequent team, under Gary Van Hee, recovered his lifeless form.

As the chaplain exhorts the group not to grieve but to pray for the Great Jumpmaster's protection of their comrade's soul, the thoughts of many of the group drift to other places, other actions, and other services. The veterans of *Desert Storm* looks back over the madness of the past weeks which characterized the operations in the desert.

Hanging back a little from the rest of the mourners, a grizzled old warrior remembers similar services after such operations—code-named *Desert 1*, *Urgent Fury*, or *Just Cause*—and drifts further back in time to days before he left Smoke Bomb Hill to join DELTA at the old stockade. His thoughts go back to the Green Beret Parachute Club, its cold beer, warm friendships and the old jukebox nestled in the corner next to the pool tables. He smiles to himself as he remembers that one song, a song from an unpopular war that saw so many of the special operations community answer the requirements of the ultimate test. Though not all of the DELTA troopers were initially Special Forces-qualified, most ended with that qualification, and an old war song expressed best the thoughts and feelings of this moment: "Her Green Beret has met his fate."

It's not all glory and gunsmoke in the realm of special operations—especially in covert operations. It can be boring for months at a time and then spiked with moments of sheer gut-wrenching, piss-in-your-pants horror. But that is what they signed up for. No yellow ribbons, no victory parades, or grand celebrations would greet these secret warriors. Just a gentle hug, a kind word, or a pat on the back that seemed to say, "Well done." That, plus "Clean up your gear and get ready for the next one!"

And there will certainly be a next one—somewhere, sometime. The odds are that the professionals from DELTA will be used not as they were during Iraq's stinging defeat, but in their traditional counterterrorist role.

For over a quarter of a century, the former Soviet Union and its surrogates in Eastern Europe, Latin America, and the Middle East gave safe haven to the world's most dangerous international terrorists. The collapse of Soviet communism, coupled with the shutting off of the terrorist's revenue by oil-rich Persian Gulf states angered over their backing of Iraq, have left terrorist organizations in disarray. Increasingly isolated politically and cut off from training and supplies from Europe and money from the Gulf, they bicker among themselves over how best to satisfy their grudge against the West and any Middle Eastern government unappreciative of their past deeds. They are, to put it bluntly, out of work and out of cash.

But the breather this has given the West is likely to be short–lived. As the world speeds toward the twenty–first century, it finds itself with more wild cards in its deck of nations. The familiar bipolar dominance of the United States and the former Soviet Union is gone for good, as the "evil empire" disintegrates into numerous successor states of questionable stability. These new countries are, themselves, not homogeneous entities and are likely to be rent by factional fighting in the decade to come. They are also the inheritors of at least 27,000 nuclear weapons. Despite pronouncements of their good intentions, their desperate need for hard currency and sporadic control of their own territory may result in some leakage of nuclear weapons ("loose nukes") or, more likely, nuclear materials and production expertise into the hands of terrorists.

This threat to peace and a new, ghastly form of warfare—environmental terrorism—may also cause elite counterterrorist units like DELTA to re-tool their operational methods. The sight of mas-sive oil slicks released on the Persian Gulf and black clouds boiling up from oil fires to shut off the noonday sun will not be lost on the next gen-eration of would–be terrorists. Moreover, their twisted logic will lead some terrorists to use the re-sults of Desert Storm to add fuel to whatever cause is fashionable at the moment.

Literally dozens of captured Palestinian and Shiite terrorists have been dumped into this cauldron of change, let loose by the Iraqis when they invaded Kuwait or released by the Israelis as part of the package deal that freed a handful of Western hostages. Like the wandering free–lance warriors of feudal Japan who traded their violent skills for gold and fame, these modern–day ronin are available to any would–be despot or group fanning the flames of ethnic or religious unrest across Eu-rope, Asia, and the Middle East. Key terrorist net-works remain intact, and a number of groups and individuals dropped from sight when the vigilance of America's intelligence assets were directed to combat in the Gulf. Now that the flex of security operations has fallen to its normal lull, the specter of terrorists finding new work in the developing chaos is very real and Americans abroad are, as always, notoriously easy targets for any group desiring big headlines.

The pros of DELTA are ready.

Index

Abu Nidal (Sabri Khalik al–Banna): 23
Achille Lauro: 71
Afghanistan: 97
Alliance For Progress: 6
American Broadcasting Company News: 67–68
Amman:23, 27; US Embassy in: 27
Arafat, Yasir: 21
Arar Royal Military Airfield: 117
Baathists: 93
Baghdad: 93
Banadah: 117
Bay of Pigs: 13
Beckwith, Colonel Charlie A: 17, 25, 30–31, 31, 61, 63–64
Beirut: 61, 70; Beirut International Airport:22; US Embassy in:70; US Marine barracks in: 69–70, 69
Berlin:74; Berlin Wall: 74–75
Bishop, Maurice: 65
Buckley, William: 73
Buraydah: 101n
Bush, President George: 93, 113
Cable News Network: 69
Cairo: 17, 22
Camp Dawson: 44
Camp David Accords: 63
Camp Troy:25, 44
Carter, President Jimmy: 13, 27, 29, 61, 63, 94
Castro, Fidel: 6
Christian militia: 69
Cold War: 6, 127
Comandancia: 76, 77
Corsica: 25
Cuba: 6, 13, 65
Curacao: 73
Czechoslovakia: 26, 104n
Dasht–e Karir: 17, 78
Dawson Field: 23
Defense Authorization Act of 1987: 79
DELTA, 1st Special Forces Operational Detachment: 6–7, 29–31, 63; chain of command: 50, 61–62; close quarters battle training: 50,–51, 53–59; investigations of: 73; news media and: 61, 67–68, 69, 98; organization: 29, 64; psychological testing: 46–47; recruitment: 41–42; selection process:41–47; training:47–59, 64, 67, 75; weapons and equipment:11, 16, 32–39, 32–38, 48, 51, 52, 56–57, 66, 75, 89, 107–109, 112, 114–115, 115
DELTA operations: antihijacking/hostage rescues:73–74; Desert Storm: 94, 98, 117, 125–127; Eagle Claw (see also Desert I and Holloway Report): 9–19, 27, 29, 63–64, 78; Honey Badger:63; Just Cause:76, 77, 126; 1984 Summer Olympics: 61, 73; 1986 Statue of Liberty Centennial: 61, 73; Urgent Fury: 65–68, 126
DePuy, General William: 29
Desert I: 9–13, 11, 17, 48, 64, 70, 78, 101, 126
Desert II: 17–18
Dhahran: 19, 94, 119
Dozier, General James L.: 68, 69
Druz militia: 69
East Germany: 74–75
Egypt: 17, 18, 21, 63, 71, 72, 98 (see also Qena Wadi)

Entebbe Airport: 24, 27
Europe: 21–22, 127
1st Bataillon de Parachutistes de Choc: 25
Fort Benning: 13, 44
Fort Bragg: 25, 30–31, 43–44, 46–47, 94, 99
Fort Campbell: 48, 81
Fort Rupert: 65
France: 24, 25, 70, 74
Frankfurt: 27, 28
Garmsar: 17
Government House: 66
Great Britain: 29, 66, 74, 93, 96; Parachute Regiment:30; Royal Air Force:23, 111 (see also London and Special Air Service)
"Great Satan": 19, 63
Green Beret Parachute Club: 126
Grenada: 63, 65–68
Grenzschutzgruppe 9: 24, 26, 32, 39, 41, 62, 63
Groupe d'Intervention de la Grendarmerie National: 24
Habbash, George: 21
Hashemite: 21
Healy, General Michael: 30
Heidelberg: 27
Higgins, Colonel William: 73
Holloway, Admiral James L.: 63
Holloway Report: 48, 63, 78, 94
Hunter Army Airfield: 81
Hussein, Saddam: 93, 95, 97–98, 109, 113, 116
Hussein, King, ibn–Talal: 21–22
Indian Ocean: 11
International Red Cross: 16
Iran: 71, 74, 97; US hostage crisis: 9–19, 94 (see also Teheran and Revolutionary Guards)
Iraq: 29, 93–94, 96–98, 109, 112, 117, 123
Israel: 21, 24, 26, 69, 98, fn98, 113
Ivory Coast, Operation: 15
Japan: 127
Johnson, Colonel Jessie: 94–95, 98–99
Jones, General David C.: 63
Jordan: 21–23, 27 (see also Amman)
Kennedy, President John F.: 6
Kenya: 26
Khomeini, Ayatollah: 9, 17
King Fahd International Airport: 94
King Khalid Military City: 101, 101n, 102, 110, 113
Kingston, Major General Robert: 30–31
Korea: 31–80
Kroesen, General Frederick J.: 30, 72
Kuwait: 29, 71, 93–94, 120, 127; US Embassy in: 94
Kuwaiti Theater of Operations: 98–99
La Belle discotheque: 74, 74
Laos: 15
Latin America: 6, 53, 65, 126
Lebanon: 22, 69–70, 69, 73
Libya: 27, 74
Lindsay, General James: 30
London:2; Iranian Embassy in: 24, 39
Los Angeles: 61, 73
MacKull, Major General Jack: 31
Malta: 72
Manila: 73
Manzariyeh Air Base: 16, 18
Meadows, Dick: 15–19
Mediterranean Sea/area: 27, 68
Meyer, Lieutenant General Edward C.: 29–30, 64
Middle East: 16, 22, 53, 95, 102, 126–127
Misirah Island: 16–18
Modelo Prison: 76
Mogadishu Airport: 24, 29, 32, 39

Montell, Colonel Robert: 31
Mubarak, President Hosni: 98
Munich Olympics: 27, 23, 27
Muse, Kurt: 76
Nairobi: 26
Nellis Air Force Base: 44
Netanyahu, Colonel Jonathan: 26
New York: 61, 73
Nimitz, USS: 9, 11, 17–18, 19
Noriega, Manuel: 76, 81
North Atlantic Treaty Organization: 68, 101
North Vietnam: 15, 15n; Paris Peace Accords, 15n
Oman: 17, 99n
Pakistan: 71
Palestinians: 21–22, 69, 71–72, 127
Panama: 76, 81
Panamanian Defence Force: 75
Peoples Revolutionary Armed Forces: 66–67
Persian Gulf: 18, 81, 94, 97, 114, 126–127
Philippines: 74
Phoenix Program: 13
Point Salines: 66
Potter, Colonel Richard: 70
Qena, Wadi: 17, 18–19
Ranch, The: 75n, 99
Reagan, President Ronald: 63, 65
Republican Guard: 93
Revolutionary Guard: 9, 13, 15, 17–19, 69
Revolutionary Military Counsel: 65
Rhein–Main Air Base: 21, 61, 71
Richardson, Lieutenant General Sir Charles: 25, 25
Rogers, General Bernard: 29–31, 61, 66
Richmond Hill Prison: 66
Sadat, Anwar: 63
San Salvador: 73
Saudi Arabia: 17, 19, 93–94, 9697, 98n, 101n, 103, 110, 120; Royal Saudi Air Force: 110–111
Schwarzkopf, General H. Norman: 95, 98
SEAL (Sea–Air–Land) teams: 53, 64; SEAL Team 6: 66–67, 71–72, 73
Secord, General Richard: 63
Shalikashville, Colonel Othan: 30
Shiite militia: 69–70, 127
Sigonella Naval Air Station: 71
Singlaub, Major General John: 63
Six Day War: 21
Smoke Bomb Hill: 30, 44, 99, 126
Soldier of Fortune: 76
Somalia: 24, 32
Son Tay Raid: 15
Soviet Union: 21, 65, 68, 72, 85, fn94, 97, 126–127
Special Air Service: 15, 24, 24–25, 29, 30, 38–39, 39, 43–44, 53, 64, 98, 99n; 22nd SAS: 25; exchange programs with DELTA/ Special Forces: 25, 53, 64
Sun Tzu: 46
Swiss Air: 19
Syria: 21, 69, 74
Tal, Premier Wafsi: 22
Task Force 160: see 160th Special Operations Aviation Regiment (Airborne)
Teheran: 9–15, 13, 15, 17; Freedom Square: 15; Mehrabad International Airport: 15, 18–19; Ministry of Foreign Affairs in: 15–18; US Embassy in 9, 11, 15–19
Tel Aviv: 98
Terrorist organizations:Abu Nidal Organization:23; Arab Revolutionary Brigades: 23; Badder–Meinhoff Gang: 23, 27; Black June Organization: 23; Black September: 22, 23; Fatah: 21, 22, 27; Fatah Revolutionary

Council: 23; Palestine Liberation Organization:21–23, 71, 74; Popular Front for the Liberation of Palestine: 21; Red Army Faction: 27, 28, 71, 72; Red Brigade: 69 (see also Revolutionary Guards); Revolutionary Military Council: 65; Revolutionary Organization of Socialist Muslims: 23
Thailand: 25, 30
Thunderbolt, Operation: 24, 29
Trans World Airlines: 22, 70–71
Tunisia: 71
Turner, Admiral Stansfield: 13–14
Uganda: 24, 26
United States: 21, 26, 68, 93, 127; Air Force: 16, 79–80, 85, 101, 110, 113, 115–116, 120, 122; Army: 29, 38, 79, 86; Central Intelligence Agency: 13, 15–16; Congress: 7, 80; Federal Bureau of Investigation: 61, 73; Justice Department: 61; Marine Corps: 38, 56, 69, 69, 70, 79; National Command Authority: 50, 62, 94; Navy: 53, 64, 66, 68, 78, 79–80 (see also SEAL teams); State Department: 13, 27, 56, 61, 69, 79; White House: 27, 29, 61, 94, 98; US Air Force Units: 8th Special Operations Squadron: 17; 1st Special Operations Wing: 99, 119 (see also United States, Air Force); 435th Tactical Air Wing: 28; Berlin hasty response team: 74–75, 75; Blue Light: 29, 31; Business Security International: 73; Command and General Staff College: 42; Corps of Engineers: fn101; XVIII Airborne Corps: 30, 99; 82d Airborne Division: 41, 94, 99; 1/245th Aviation Regiment (Special Operations, Airborne): 81; 5th Special Forces Group: 25, 32; 1st Corps Support Command: 99; 1st Ranger Battalion: 81; Forces Command: 30; 509th Airborne Infantry: 27; Intelligence Support Activity: 64, 73, 94; John F. Kennedy Special Warfare Center: 30–31, 45, 125; Joint Casualty Resolution Center: 30; 160th Special Operations Aviation Regiment (Airborne): 48, 56, 65–67, 76, 77, 79, 81, 82, 87, 99; Rangers: 16, 18, 29, 31, 44, 50, 95; 75th Ranger Regiment: 94; 7th Special Forces Group:25; 617th Special Operations Aviation Detachment: 81; 6th Infantry Regiment: 75; Special Forces: 16, 25, 27, 30–31, 43–44, 63, 73, 105, 113, 114, 126; Special Forces School: 30; Special Operations Command: 30, 50, 79; Special Operations Training Facility: 46, 47–49, 48, 49, 54, 61, 64, (also see Wally World and the Ranch); 10th Special Forces Group: 30, 56, 70; Training and Doctrine Command: 29; US Army, Europe: 27, 69, 72; West Point: 31; (see also United States, Army and DELTA): Central Command: 94–95, 98, 110; Joint Chief of Staff: 50, 62–63, 95; Joint Special Operations Command: 48, 50, 62, 64, 94; Joint Task Force: 13, 15–17; Special Operations Command, Central Command: 94, 110, 114, 116, 122
Unit 269: 26, 26
Venezuala: 73
Vietnam War: 13–15, 21, 31, 85, 91, 119
Vought, Major General James B.: 13
Wally World: 64, 75n, 76
Warsaw Pact: 104n
Wegener, Colonel Ulrich: 26, 32
West Germany: 16–17, 23–24, 27, 29, 61, 72 (see also Grenzschutzgruppe 9)
Willemstad: 73
Yom Kippur: 21